INVISIBLE IMPRINT

What Others Feel
When In Your Presence

Understanding
the forces of
Good and Evil

Dr. Richard D. Dobbins

Published by VMI Publishers, Sisters, Oregon

Unless otherwise indicated, all Scripture quotations are taken from the Holy Bible, New International Version (NIV), copyright 1973, 1978, 1979 by International Bible Society; Scripture quotations marked NKJV are taken from the New King James Version copyright by Thomas Nelson Publishers. Scripture quotations marked NLT are taken from the New Living Translation, copyright 1996 by Tyndale House Publishers.

Printed in the United States of America

ISBN 0-9712311-1-7

Published by VMI Publishers, Sisters, Oregon

CONTENTS

To my wife, Priscilla, whose loving presence has left a deep and lasting imprint on my life. Without her encouragement and persistent protection I would not have been able to complete this project.

Acknowledgments

In preparing this book for publication I found myself indebted to many people. The creative help of my editors, Bill and Nancie Carmichael, has been invaluable. Their suggestions have kept the book sharply focused and relevant to the reader. I depended greatly on Mrs. Wandalee Rader, my administrative assistant and Mrs. Carol Adams, my copy editor for the preparation of the manuscript. Dr. Donald Lichi, Dr. Richard Serbin, Rev. Carl Miller, Rev. Derrill Sharp, Dr. Kathryn Wurtz, and my wife were kind enough to read an early draft of the book and offer many constructive criticisms. I am indebted to my graduate students for allowing me to refine the thoughts of the book through a series of lectures to which I subjected them. Kenny and Mary Ann King, often relieved me of guilt when I had to put other obligations aside temporarily to work on the book. Michael and Jacquie Caroone and Danny Benvenuti were kind enough to provide me with the privacy of their homes for completing the manuscript. My wife, Priscilla, has been a constant source of encouragement to me in this project.

Forward

Most normal people want "Good" to prevail. That's the reason we love to go to movies that always show the good guy winning. It's the reason Star Wars was such a huge hit. Good overcomes evil, right corrects wrong, and truth wins out. And it's true for more than just movies. Something in the heart of most human beings yearns for goodness and truth. History shows us that ultimately, the forces of good do overcome the forces of evil.

That is not to say the evil does not keep trying to prevail or that it does not have its day in human history. The events of September 11, 2001 have changed our lives forever. Thousands of people were lost and a way of life lost with it.

We all watched in horror the presence of Evil being played out as airplane following airplane crashed into those gleaming towers turning a beautiful fall morning into dark clouds of choking rubble. And then we watched in awe the presence of Good being played out as hero after hero performed amazing feats to save the lives of others and minister hope and healing. It seems that wherever Evil gouges out a hole in the surface of history, eventually Good comes along and fills it with life sustaining water again.

Terrorists are not the first ones to wreak havoc on the world. For several millenniums, Good and Evil have been at war. Evil has raised its ugly head many times in the history of mankind.... men like Hitler and Usama bin Laden are undeniable proof. But history also has its St. Francis of Assisi's, Abraham Lincoln's and Mother Teresa's. And there are millions more, lesser known than these.

In the end, the Bible tells us that Truth wins, that Christ's victory shall be fully realized, and those who put their trust in Him do indeed prevail. But what most of us do not realize is how our own sense of presence makes its impact on those around us right now. Frankly, I had not given much thought about how this plays out in my own life until I read this manuscript. While I knew

I had influence (my wife and kids can tell you how much I try to super-impose my influence on others)... I had never really thought about "presence" in the way Doc describes in this book ("Doc," by the way, is a pet name for Dr. Dobbins that those of us who know him affectionately use). Like the now actors on the stage of life, it is our turn in history to express Good and Evil by engaging ourselves in the war for truth and virtue.

The words of Jesus, when telling us to "Lay up treasures in heaven where moth and rust do not corrupt" have taken on new meaning for me. I realize that I am making significant "deposits" into the lives of others every time I walk into their presence or they walk into mine. And it happens every day with each of us.

Remember the saying we used to say when we were kids, "sticks and stones may break my bones, but words can never hurt me?" Well, in many ways that's not true. Words do hurt sometimes. Words are creative. Words influence the "deposits" we make on other people. Words come from the heart. (The Bible tells us, "Out of the abundance of the heart the mouth speaks.") Your "presence" on the lives of your children, your spouse, your friends, your co-workers are profound indeed.

The "invisible imprints" that shape us and ultimately help shape others around us are making their mark every day, whether we like it or not. There is no neutral ground here. Like radio signals, these impressions are being picked up, read, interpreted, and deposited on the hearts and minds of the people we contact. And we are making daily choices about which "force" we let into our own mind and spirit.

We all know people we love to be around. For you, it might be a parent or teacher who has inspired you or mentored you. It might be a grandparent who shows unconditional love toward you. How do you feel about those people who have deposited rich resources of love, wisdom, knowledge, kindness and discipline into your life? If you're like me, you feel blessed to know them. You hope someday to be something like them.

For me, it was many people. But one man stands out

above the rest. His name was Earl Book. He was a man who was so close to Almighty God, when I was in his presence, I knew I was also in the presence of Jesus. Earl was a little guy, maybe five feet, six inches tall. But his "presence" was gigantic. Earl died last year, but I can still sense his presence and the "deposits" he made in my life.

My goal is to be like Earl to somebody. I am working on developing that kind of presence with my grandkids. Whether or not I get there remains to be seen. But I know that the invisible imprints I make now will carry on far beyond my last breath. May God help me to get it right...to leave footprints that lead them toward Good.

I am honored that Doc would let me write the forward to the wonderful concepts he presents in such clear form in this book.

William Carmichael, speaker and author of *"Seven Habits of a Healthy Home,"* and *"Lord, Bless My Child."*

Introduction

Like footprints in the sand, imprints reveal their origin. The massive footprints of a dinosaur once imbedded in volcanic ash as well as the delicate fronds of a fern frozen in stone become unique monuments to their source.

The sculptor understands this principle. When he wants to capture the likeness of a person in bronze he first makes a mask from the imprint of the person's face in plaster. Once the imprint is permanently set it becomes a mold from which the bust is cast. The imprint produces the likeness.

Throughout our lives, in much more subtle and profound ways, you and I leave living invisible imprints that help to shape the people with whom we interact in life...and they leave their imprints on us. These unique impressions planted firmly in our minds and fixed in our memories make a lasting contribution to our identity. They can be hurtful or helpful.

This book makes us aware of those invisible imprints and how they are formed. Not only do people affect us, but the forces of good and evil also leave their marks on us. My hope is to heighten your awareness of this whole invisible process and help you become more conscious of the way others feel when in your presence.

If we think about it, all of us can recall people whose presence has left an invisible imprint on our lives. Because our fear of pain is more essential to our survival than our desire for pleasure, we are likely to remember our villains, the people who have hurt us, more quickly than we can recall our heroes, those who have helped us. On the other hand, since we do not like to think that we are responsible for anyone's pain, we may recall more easily the people who have been helped by our imprint than those we have hurt.

Often, our recollections of pain and the anger it provokes wrap themselves like fangs deeply embedded around our hurtful memories refusing to let us be free from them. Until God helps us confront these memories of our past the poison buried there will continue to infect our present and threaten our future. Once we have had the courage to lance these pockets of infection and grace has cleansed the wounds we can put ourselves beyond the reach of the people whose imprints have hurt us and move forward with our lives. Throughout the book you will find practical suggestions for helping you do this.

However, the main purpose of this book is to make us aware of the invisible imprint we are leaving on the lives of others. What do other people feel when they are in our presence? Increased awareness of this hidden process will help us to leave the kind of invisible imprint on the lives of others that will be a blessing to them and bring glory to God.

CHAPTER ONE

EVERY PERSON HAS A PRESENCE

Standing on the rim of the Grand Canyon and gazing out over those millions of acres of gutted rock, we find ourselves wondering how long it took the surging waters of the Colorado River cascading through that canyon to erode that much rock. Hushed by the awe of it all, we become aware of the unique presence of the Creator.

In contrast, standing at the edge of the ghoulish looking tombstone-like outside walls swaying over the six-story pile of rubble where the World Trade Towers once proudly stood stunningly confirms the unmistakable presence of evil in our world. Emergency vehicles, stretchers and body bags make us shutter with the awareness of such a diabolical reality.

These contrasts symbolize the battle being waged between God and Satan for control of this planet. Through our choices, to one degree or another, each of us becomes a bodily expression of a "presence."

Standing in the Lincoln Memorial one feels the presence of a man who had a profound influence on our nation. The sculptor has portrayed a haunting melancholy look on the face of the sixteenth President of the United States. One imagines what steady resolve he must have had to steer our nation through the great crisis of the Civil War.

As you read the stirring words of Abraham Lincoln's second inaugural address engraved on the walls there, this unique presence intensifies. The silence that sweeps over you seems so appropriate it goes unnoticed.

For good or evil, for greatness or commonness, as somebody's hero or villain, every person has a presence.

I discovered this many years ago, as a six-year-old boy, when I entered Miss Kaller's first grade classroom. She was an elderly teacher who never married. Her whole life had been devoted to children. I was blessed that she had not been forced to retire when she reached the age of sixty-five.

When I entered her class she was in her early seventies. Her hair was thinning. The coarse blue veins in her elderly hands were readily visible through her paper-thin skin. I still remember her kindly penetrating blue eyes and the dignified look on her narrow angular face as she stood tall and straight to address the class.

There was something majestic about her presence that made us first-graders feel someone very important and intelligent cared about us and believed that we could learn. She taught us the Pledge of Allegiance, the Ten Commandments, the twenty-third Psalm, the one hundredth Psalm. We learned the alphabet and various ways each letter could sound.

She played recordings of great symphony orchestras and taught us to identify the various instruments by their sound. I still benefit from the sense of rhythm she ingrained in me by letting me play various instruments in the rhythm band.

When I was in Miss Kaller's presence I wanted to behave. I wanted to study and learn. I cared about what she thought of me because I knew she loved me and I wanted to please her. Sixty-five years later the imprint of her presence is still vivid in my memory. Her name ranks high on the list of people who have had a profoundly positive impact on my life.

What Is Presence?

Presence is a common experience, but also a mystical one. You can't see it, but you can feel it. It is invisible, but not intangible. Presence is the invisible impact you feel when you are around certain people, places, or things.

Every person has a presence! Your presence is the most enduring part of your life. It leaves traces of you like an invisible imprint on everyone you meet in life, especially on those who are the closest to you. Everyone who encounters you feels your presence when they are around you. And, no one else has a presence exactly like yours.

The Spirit/Mind and Brain

The presence emanating from you is produced through a very complex process continually occurring in your mind and brain. Your brain has an unbelievable capacity for storing multidimensional memories from your past. For example, I can still see my grandmother standing at her kitchen counter mixing the dough for her famous cinnamon rolls. Beads of perspiration would break into streams down her narrow forehead as she rolled the dough into thin sheets. Although it has been over sixty years ago, I can still recall the smell of yeast from freshly rising dough as though it were yesterday. As the rolls were carefully put on baking sheets and placed in a pre-heated oven the unforgettable aroma of hot brown sugar and cinnamon filled the house. I remember the feel of the big ceramic mixing bowl held tightly between my left arm and my stomach as I energetically scraped the sides with a tablespoon gripped firmly in my right hand determined to leave as little of the warm glazed icing there as possible. I remember how slowly the time seemed to pass before the rolls were done and I could sink my teeth into the finished product.

Your brain is also filled with memories from your history, carefully stored there by your mind. All these sensations (the sights, sounds, feelings, smells, and tastes) are kept in different parts of the brain and are inexplicably orchestrated by your mind or spirit when you want to recall them so that these memories can be relived just as you have chosen to remember them. Out of this complex process comes the version of your life you believe to be true.

As you can see, our presence is profoundly affected by the way we have chosen to remember our past. Later we will discover that God has a creative version of your memories that will comfort you and bring peace to your mind or spirit in the event you are troubled by your past. And, Satan has a destructive version of those same events that can leave you feeling anxious and depressed.

Becoming Aware of Your World

God has designed our mind and brain to be the place where the invisible world of spiritual reality and the natural world of physical reality interface. In His conversation with Nicodemus, a Jewish leader, Jesus uses the analogy of physical birth to explain the necessity of a spiritual birth.[1] He reminded Nicodemus that until we are physically born we are only vaguely aware of the great big, wide, and wonderful world outside our mother. Our prenatal world is limited to the sounds and feelings we are exposed to while still a part of our mother's body. However, physical birth brings us into direct contact with the physical world and enables us to begin interacting meaningfully with it.

Jesus tried to help Nicodemus understand that just as physical birth equips you to interact with the physical world in a meaningful way, once you are spiritually born ("born again"), your spirit or mind equips you to interact with the invisible world of spiritual presence in meaningful ways.

In later chapters we will discover this "invisible world" is comprised of an interesting and powerful variety of sources from which spiritual presence comes. In addition to your unique presence, there is the presence of Good and Evil, expressed through God, Satan, angels, and demons...all very real and powerful. But you are unique in that you have the freedom to choose what role each of these will play in defining your "presence."

A person unfamiliar with spiritual realities may feel somewhat uncomfortable about seriously considering the possibility of an "invisible world" affecting their presence. But think of the many invisible sources of physical power we have come to rely on already in the normal pursuit of everyday life: electricity, sound waves, light waves, electro-magnetic fields, solar power, and nuclear energy. We take these invisible sources of power for granted and have grown so dependent on them it is difficult for us to imagine what our daily lives would be without them.

Just as science has developed the technology to put such invisible sources of power at our disposal, so God has equipped our spirit/mind to interface with these invisible sources of spiritual power. Our brain is the physical organ that becomes the battlefield on which spiritual warfare is waged between our spirit and the forces of Good and Evil to determine whose presence will be expressed through our body. Like a television is equipped with the technical ability to intercept and translate a select program of invisible waves of light and sound into visible pictures and audible sounds, so through your mental processes you are spiritually equipped to intercept a select set of *spiritual impressions* and translate them into *physical expressions.* As the television set becomes an extension of your eyes and ears enabling you to choose to see and hear programs that would otherwise remain invisible and inaudible to you, so your spirit becomes an extension of your brain enabling you to experience urges, fantasies and ideas that are spiritually stimulated. Some of these are from God, and some from Satan. They are to be distinguished from natural urges, fantasies, and ideas related to our physical survival.

However, in making these distinctions, it is necessary to remember that Satan can use any of our natural urges to seriously impair, or even destroy our lives. For example, something as innocent as breathing can provoke the use of exhilarating, but potentially deadly inhalants.

The ability to translate urges, fantasies, and ideas into attitudes and behavior is a unique gift God has reserved exclusively for human beings. This is what sets us apart from all other creatures. Only human beings can give visible physical expression to the invisible presence of spirit beings. This is why it is so important that we develop the wisdom to discern the origin of our urges, fantasies, and ideas as early in the decision-making process as possible. Unfortunately, very few of us are taught the skill of making these kinds of spiritual discriminations in our youth. Later, we will delve more deeply into the issues at stake in the war between Good and Evil and the role we have in that conflict. You will see how deeply your response to Good or Evil affects the presence projected from your life and consequently the way others respond to you. But for now let's take a closer look at this whole idea of presence and the process that produces it.

Your Physical Presence

Most of us are concerned about our physical presence. Often our status and influence are enhanced or diminished because of it. Our physical appearance reflects on our family. So, the importance of giving attention to how we look and act in public begins very early in our lives.

As soon as we are old enough to recognize brand names we want our parents to buy us the shoes or clothes our popular classmates wear. As we grow older this interest in the fashion world continues to play an important role in defining our physical appearance. When we meet with our peers we want to be sure that we are dressed to command their attention and respect. Style and fads become the norm because most of us care about what people think of our physical appearance. Even some who dress shabbily or lack habits of cleanliness or grooming, are often sending a physical "statement" about who they are.

Spiritual Presence Is More Important

We tend to focus much more on our physical appearance than we do on our spiritual presence. Many people are unaware of their spiritual presence. They don't even know they have one. For example, some people behave obnoxiously in public and either don't know, or don't care that other people find their presence offensive.

The irony is that these same people who have no idea what other people feel when they are around them, are often acutely aware of what they feel when they are around other people. And, they don't hesitate to lash out at them when they find their behavior irritating or unpleasant.

As you can see, we tend to be more aware of the feelings other people generate in us than we are of the feelings we generate in them. If we are going to be more in touch with the impact our presence has on the feelings of others, it is important for us to understand that our outward attitudes and behavior are almost always a product of our inner spirit. Jesus said, "Out of the abundance of our heart, our mouth speaks."[2]

What Do People Feel When They Are Around You?

People respond to the spiritual and emotional overflow of our lives. Whatever dominates our inner life motivates our interaction with other people and stimulates their reactions to us. By becoming aware of the feelings you experience when you are around other people you can learn much about the spiritual and emotional overflow of their lives. And, by noticing how they react to you, you can make some important discoveries about the spiritual and emotional overflow of your own life.

To help you become more aware of the nature of your presence and that of those you meet, here are six common personality types and how people are likely to feel around them.

1. Angry People

Can you recall how you felt the last time you were with an adult who was really mad or angry? They create a very uncomfortable feeling in others, even when you are not the person with whom they are angry. Everyone in their presence feels their anger.

They have an angry presence. We don't like to be around them. If we can avoid them socially we will.

When we have to be around angry people we are likely to feel both anxious and angry about having to tolerate a person whose presence makes us so uncomfortable. You feel like you can't express yourself for fear of triggering their anger. Trying to find the right words to use in talking with them is like trying to walk across a floor full of freshly cracked eggshells without getting any yolk on your feet.

2. Overly Sensitive People

Most of us are just as uncomfortable around overly sensitive people. We fear saying or doing something that may offend them. We're on needles and pins when we are around them so we try to avoid them as much as possible. Of course, overly sensitive people pick up on this and become even more sensitive. They become more convinced that people don't like them. And, they are totally unaware of generating feelings that make them difficult to like. The way they have chosen to respond to a history of rejection predisposes them to a future of rejection.

3. Anxious People

Anxious people are pre-occupied with their fears. The world has become so threatening to them that even when they are physically present with you they are emotionally remote. Whatever relationship you have with them is going to be shallow and superficial because they are so emotionally over-invested in trying to be sure they are safe. Often you find yourself feeling sorry for these people. However, if you attempt to reassure them they may become very dependent on you and that will create a different kind of discomfort for you. So, remember, until they deal effectively with their anxiety they will have very little to invest in a healthy friendship with you.

4. Critical People

Critical people are usually finding fault with someone or something. Otherwise, they have very little to say.

In many cases, these people were never able to live up to the unrealistic expectations of perfectionist parents. Therefore, they find some kind of sick relief in drawing attention to the imperfections of others. As strange as it may seem, their merciless criticism of others is nothing compared to the severe demands they place on themselves.

People who frequently criticize leave us with few options. Remaining silent may leave them with the false impression that we agree with them. Challenging their opinions will likely produce a long-unpleasant confrontation because they usually insist on defending their opinions.

5. Overbearing People

Overbearing people are determined to hold center stage wherever they are. They dominate every conversation. Whatever you have done, they have done better. Wherever you have gone, they've been there more often and stayed at nicer places. Most people find this kind of verbal one-upsmanship obnoxious and boring, but the overbearing person is unaware he or she is generating such feelings in others.

The overbearing person is self-consumed. Often, as children, they have been over-indulged by parents and grandparents. Unfortunately, they assume others are still as interested in their exploits as those who indulged them as children.

6. Pessimistic People

Pessimistic people see the dark side of everything and want to dump it on others. Show them a glass half full of water and they see it half empty. Show them a donut and they see the hole. You are reluctant to let them know you feel good because you don't want to make them feel worse.

Often, pessimistic people are attempting to protect themselves from disappointment and their fear of failure. Although a person's expectations of life should be realistic, a pessimistic view of life leaves a person very vulnerable to depression.

While we could highlight other attitudes that create a negative presence, one thing most of these people would have in common is that they don't have a clue as to the nature of their "presence" and how it affects others when they are around them. They are so out of touch with their own presence they wouldn't know themselves if they met themselves walking down the street. They are also unaware of any connection between their presence and the choices they have made in the past...and are continuing to make. They don't have the slightest idea of how they came to be the way they are.

On the other hand, each of us can recall people in our lives whose presence has been like an oasis in the desert. They always seem to have something refreshing to share. We are blessed by their faith, their optimism, their creativity, their curiosity, their courage, their ambition, their transparency, and their honesty. During the scorching heat of personal trials friends like these hover over you allowing their presence to become like the cool shade of a long shadow attended by a refreshing breeze.

What Kind of Presence Do You Have?

How would other people describe the "vibes" they get when they are around you? You can begin to get in touch with their feelings by asking yourself a series of questions like: How do I feel about the person I am with when I am alone? How do others feel when I enter their presence? How does my spouse feel with I come home from work? Is he/she anticipating or dreading our being together? How do those I love feel when they know I am on my way to be with them? Does my presence excite, bore, frighten, antagonize, overwhelm, depress, or anger those I love? What do my fellow workers feel when I am around them? How would they characterize my presence? Are they guarded, or worried when I am with them? Or does my presence affirm, inspire, encourage, and uplift them?

Such introspection can spur in us a new commitment to become more like the kind of person that brings out the best in others, and draws others toward us rather than repels them from us. Becoming more aware of our presence and the impact we have on others is the first step toward taking better control of it. On the next page you will find *The Personal Presence Rating Scale* I have designed to help put you in touch with what others feel when you are with them. Feel free to copy it. Make copies for your spouse or a family member, a close personal friend, and a fellow worker. Be sure they understand the instructions and assure them that you want them to be completely honest in their responses.

How Is Presence Formed?

Your presence is the product of your choices over time. Notice, your presence is produced; it is not pre-determined. And, you are the one who produces it. How? By your choices. For better or for worse, each of us is responsible for our own choices. Over time, our choices produce our presence.

Very early in life, we begin to make significant choices that affect the nature and intensity of our presence. The ways we go about making our choices gradually develop into identifiable and predictable patterns that become an important part of our personality and character structure. This process occurs so subtly we are unaware of its formative influence on us.

Let's divide our "choices" into two types: First, the choices we make in determining how we will view and respond to the things that happen to us over which we have little or no control, I call *Interpretive Choices*. Second, the conscious and unconscious choices we make in matters we do have some control over. These are our *Definitive Choices*.

Personal Presence Rating Scale

Instructions: On a scale from 1 to10* rate each of the following words to indicate your impressions of how other people generally feel when in your presence. Enter each rating by the appropriate word in the column marked, "Self." Then, give copies of the rating scale to your spouse or a family member, a close friend, and a fellow worker and have them use the same scale to rate how they actually feel when they are in your presence. Be sure they enter their ratings for each word in the appropriate column across from the word.

*1=How they almost never feel when in your presence.
10=How they almost always feel when in your presence.

	Self	Spouse or Family Member	Friend	Fellow Worker
1. Affirmed	____	____	____	____
2. Criticized	____	____	____	____
3. Hopeful	____	____	____	____
4. Depressed	____	____	____	____
5. Encouraged	____	____	____	____
6. Overwhelmed	____	____	____	____
7. Loved	____	____	____	____
8. Rejected	____	____	____	____
9. Excited	____	____	____	____
10. Inferior	____	____	____	____
11. Reassured	____	____	____	____
12. Belittled	____	____	____	____
13. Enabled	____	____	____	____
14. Attacked	____	____	____	____
15. Happy	____	____	____	____
16. Irritated	____	____	____	____
17. Accepted	____	____	____	____
18. Seduced	____	____	____	____
19. Valued	____	____	____	____
20. Deceived	____	____	____	____
Totals				

Scoring: Place a minus sign (-) in front of the score for each even numbered word. Then total each column by subtracting the minus scores from the plus scores for the odd numbered words. The higher the score the more positively people feel when in your presence.

Interpretive Choices

Perhaps nothing has more to do with our presence than the things about our past we choose to remember and the things we choose to forget. Every day, this hidden and unconscious filter functions in our decision-making process and silently shapes the conscious realities of our life.

As all of us know, there are parts of our history we have had no control over. We have had no say at all in the circumstances. We did not choose our parents so we had no control over our genetics. We had no say into which family we would be born, what kind of marriage our parents would have or who our siblings would be. We did not choose our birth order, the neighborhood we grew up in, or the schools we attended. Some have had to live with illnesses, accidents, tragedies, or birth anomalies. All of these factors result in some people being called upon to bear greater burdens than others. However, no one lives a pain-free life.

If I wanted to focus only on the hurts in my history there are many reasons for me to be an angry and depressed person.

As a fifteen-year-old girl my mother married a man who sexually abused her. She divorced him when she was sixteen, so she was single when my father came into her life.

She married him when she was eighteen years old. She had me when she was nineteen. Thirteen days after I was born she died as a result of my birth. For years, I held myself as accountable for her death as I would have been had I deliberately killed her.

My mother's sister married when she was sixteen. She had a daughter when she was eighteen. The following year her husband died from tuberculosis. So my aunt was single when my mother died.

A few months after my mother's death my father married my aunt, and my cousin became my stepsister. Six years later, they had a child of their own. So I grew up in a home where it was "your kid," "my kid," and "our kid." No two of us children had the same biological parents. We had a "blended family" before sociologists could tell us what to call it.

I ran away from home and married when I was seventeen. My wife was also seventeen. When we were nineteen we had our first child. Early in the pregnancy my wife suffered from severe toxemia. Eight months and five days into gestation it was no longer safe for her or the baby to extend the pregnancy. So she had to give Cesarean section birth to our first child—a son.

I will never forget the glazed look in Dolores' eyes as I rode with her in the ambulance on the way home from the hospital. That's when she informed me that she had committed the unpardonable sin. She said she was hopelessly lost...just like Judas. She told me this several times over the next few weeks.

For several months, she was suicidal. She tried to take her life three times.

Then, our second child contracted polio. Our third child was born with a congenital heart defect that had to be corrected by open-heart surgery when she was a young adult. About the time our third child was born, I got rheumatoid arthritis. I had to have the fluid on my knees drained twice a week. My shoulders were so crippled I couldn't put on a coat or drive a car. Doctors told me I would never be free from that dreadful disease. And, today my right shoulder is still partially paralyzed from it.

What I am attempting to say is that life treats us all very much alike. Everyone's life has storms. The rains descend, the winds blow, the floods beat on everybody's house. You and I not only determine which of life's experiences we will forget and which ones we will accumulate in our memories, but we also choose the *version* of those experiences we believe to be true.

Part of our presence flows out of the ways *we choose to interpret and react to these painful events*, not produced by the events themselves. This is why I refer to these choices as "*Interpretive Choices.*"

None of us live with the facts of our lives, we live with the story we tell ourselves about those facts. That story can be crippling or creative depending on who we allow to influence our interpretation...God or Satan. Both can be very convincing. Ultimately, you and I will choose the version we will believe.

It is important to distinguish the difference between the facts of your life and your interpretation of those facts. Until we are able to make this distinction we are left to conclude that the facts and our *view of the facts are the same.*

Perhaps this lesson is most easily learned by reminding ourselves of what happens in a courtroom when two skilled lawyers are making vastly differing arguments from the same set of facts. If you have ever served on a jury you realize how differently the same set of facts can be viewed.

The prosecutor argues very persuasively for one interpretation of the facts and the defense attorney argues just as strongly for another point of view. Then, when the jury gets the case and begins to deliberate you discover there are still other ways the facts can be viewed. Finally, you arrive at an interpretation most of you believe to be true. In a way, this is similar to how each of us goes about mentally processing the events of our lives, arriving at an interpretation we choose to believe. This version results in our emotional response to the events being considered.

Particularly important are the ways we choose to react to the painful experiences of life. As I have already said, life is a mixture of pleasure and pain, burden and blessing. The rains descend, the winds blow, the floods beat on everybody's house. You and I not only determine which of life's experiences we will forget and which we will accumulate in our memories, but we also choose the version of those facts we believe to be true.

Later in this book we will discover that both God and Satan have convincing ways of interpreting these facts for you. God's versions are redemptive. Satan's are destructive.

Definitive Choices

Definitive choices are those decisions we make in circumstances where we have primary control. How we choose to respond to limits imposed on us by our parents; how we react to older and younger siblings; how we accept the routines of the family: mealtime, bedtime, bath time, etc.; the people we choose as our friends; how we interact with our friends; the habits we develop, both good and bad; these are *"Definitive Choices"* that eventually shape our character and form our presence.

Over time, our choices gradually reveal how loving or selfish; involved or withdrawn; enthusiastic or lethargic; intense or relaxed; determined or compliant; obedient or rebellious; disciplined or impulsive; optimistic or pessimistic; confrontational or congenial we will be. Where your *"Definitive Choices"* fall within these dimensions will make a profound impact on what other people feel when they are around you.

So, over time your presence is formed by how you choose to remember and respond to the things in your life over which you had no control (your *"Interpretive Choices"*); and, your conscious and unconscious choices in situations over which you have had various degrees of control (your *"Definitive Choices"*).

Here is the essence of what I am saying; *your choices determine your presence*. No one else is responsible for those choices. If you had made different choices you would have a different presence . . . for better or for worse!

Joseph Had a Choice

The Bible story of Joseph and the unjust treatment he received from his brothers provides us with a beautiful illustration of this truth.

As you will recall, Joseph's brothers were envious of him. They hated him. When they had an opportunity they sold him into slavery, killed an animal and soaked his dream-coat in the blood and as they handed this blood-stained evidence to their father, they told him that Joseph had been killed. Joseph had every right to fill his heart with hatred over the years and wait for an opportunity for revenge. That certainly would have been a justifiable choice.

Instead, Joseph chose to look for opportunities to bless and help others whether in the palace or the prison. God honored his attitude. Pharaoh chose Joseph to be Prime Minister of Egypt.

During the famine his brothers were forced to come to him for food. At first, they didn't recognize him, but when he revealed himself to them terror filled their hearts for they knew this was Joseph's opportunity for vengeance.

However, God had helped Joseph discover and superimpose upon his sale into slavery a beautiful and creative version of those facts. Joseph had not lived for vengeance. He had lived for the Lord. And the Lord gave him the grace to face his brothers with a broken and tender heart, saying to them, "...you thought evil against me; but God meant it for good."[3] While Joseph had no control over the cruel treatment of his brothers, he did choose how he would respond. And God has a similar creative way for you to look at the painful chapters of *your* history.

Satan wants to use the wounds of your life to steal your joy, rob you of peace, and destroy your life. His version of your past will poison your presence. However, God can take your painful history just like He did Joseph's and use it to give birth to a positive presence that will bless others and honor Him.

Making Spiritual Choices

Earlier, I made the point that we are not just body and soul, but spirit as well. That is the part of us that is created in the image of God. In addition to the realities of the natural world there are worlds of spiritual reality. This mostly invisible spiritual world includes the presence of Good and Evil, expressed through God, Satan, angels, and demons . . . all very real, and with powerful presence. But your choice is the deciding factor in determining the "presence" growing out of and expressed by your life. You and I make spiritual choices every day, and those choices play a vital part in how our presence is formed and expressed.

Unfortunately, sin destroyed our natural awareness of these invisible worlds, but all is not lost. In the New Testament, Jesus has a fascinating conversation with one of the Jewish leaders named Nicodemus. Remember, he illustrates how we can reconnect with the spiritual part of our being. We referred to this in Chapter One.

In the next few chapters we will be able to discover the amazing truth about how we can become spiritually alive and fully aware of God's presence in our lives. We will also discover that this battle for our presence presently raging between our ears began long before Adam and Eve were created. Although understanding the history of the battle won't win it for us, it certainly will help us fight it more wisely. In order for us to be able to fully understand our choices in shaping our spiritual presence, we need to take a look at God's presence in eternity, the fall of Lucifer and the beginning of evil, why God created Adam and Eve, and how sin entered the human race. Then we will be ready to explore ways of changing our presence, making our presence God's presence, and our presence in eternity.

FOOTNOTES

[1] John 3:1-7
[2] Matthew 12:34
[3] Genesis 50:20

CHAPTER TWO

THE
PRESENCE
OF
GOD

"...through all eternity God is the social Trinity, the community of love."[1]

Often as a boy growing up in northeastern Alabama I lay on my back in the dew-dampened grass on a clear night trying to count the stars. Inevitably, when I reached a hundred or more I forgot where I started so I began to count them all over again. Finally after two or three attempts, I gave up and just gazed into the night sky, mesmerized by it all. I wondered how far all those stars were from me; how far they were from each other, how long they had been there, and how they got there in the first place.

This experience launched my awareness of the presence of God. It would be years before I would invite Him into my life, but the wonder I encountered on those memorable nights gave such an undeniable argument for a Creator that I have never since doubted the existence of God. Today I am more in awe than ever of all He has created.

The shepherd boy David must have had feelings similar to mine when he was alone at night on the hillsides of Israel tending his father's sheep. Perhaps this is what inspired him to write:

> "O Lord, our Lord, how excellent is your name in all the earth! You have set your glory above the heavens...When I consider your heavens, the work of your fingers, the moon and the stars that you have set in place, what is man that you are mindful of him? Or, the son of man that you care for him." [2]

David's eloquence put my boyhood feelings into words. How could the Creator turn His attention away from such breathtaking things long enough to care about a little kid on the hillsides of Israel *or* northeastern Alabama? Thoughts like this still capti-vate me when I peer into a sky full of stars twinkling like diamonds against the black velvet of a moonless night.

Nature has ways of making us gasp at spectacular displays of God's beauty and power: spring's sudden burst of brilliant color, a rainbow's sparkling spectrum of sunlight filtered through rain drops, the golden glow of a harvest moon bathing an October sky, mountains of snow paralyzing and momentarily purifying our urban filth. How can a person remain unmoved when con-fronted by awesome scenes like these!

Nature Overwhelms Us With Questions

During these times we find ourselves thinking about haunting "existential" questions like:[3] Was anyone out there before creation? How did creation happen? What is it about? Are there other forms of life out there? How did life on earth begin? Why did it begin? What is life all about? And, in a more pro-foundly personal sense, *What is* my *life all about?*

Many scientific thinkers contend that there are no ulti-mate answers to these questions. According to them life has no meaning...no purpose! Creation was a serendipitous event. It simply "happened." A body of matter somewhere in space sud-denly exploded and a "Big Bang" rang out through the emptiness of eternity. These people believe from that moment on the rest of creation just somehow naturally evolved over billions of years. Still, they are unable to account for the origin of the mass or gasses involved in the "Big Bang."

Such an atheistic evolutionary approach to creation seems incredible. It not only denies any purpose in creation, but also deprives you and me of any definitive meaning in life...any reason for being. It makes us mere accidents of nature...fetuses our parents just happened not to abort. To believe something as complex as the universe and awesome as human life can happen without any involvement of intelligence or ultimate purpose stretches human imagination to the breaking point.

On the other hand, for those willing to believe, the Bible offers plausible answers to these deep and penetrating questions. These answers are found in the biblical accounts of creation; the fall of Lucifer, God's brightest and most powerful angel; the creation of Adam and Eve; their disobedience; and, God's plan of redemption for us and our planet.

How Does Eternity Impact My Life?

Eternity is timeless. It is of infinite duration. Matter is not eternal. It is temporal and essential to the existence of time. Before there was matter there could be no time because time simply measures the speed with which matter moves through space. So from God's point of view, time is relative. *"With the Lord a day is like a thousand years and a thousand years are like a day."* [4]

As time-bound creatures, it is difficult for us to grasp the reality of a point in the past when nothing existed... when there was no time. We automatically think in terms of seconds, minutes, hours, days, months, and years. Our lives are so driven by time most of us wear it on our wrist.

It rarely dawns on us that these measurements of our existence so important in our world are all artificial divisions of time that do not exist for tribal cultures. For them, time divides itself into natural events such as sunrise, sunset, the new moon, and full moon. But even these more natural ways of dividing time still depend on the speed of our planet as it plods its way around the sun. Consequently, we are all severely handicapped when trying to grasp any reality outside of the space-time world.

We only know the fleeting temporal reality in which we find ourselves at the moment. Making sense out of life while limited to such a restricted view is not easy. In some ways it is like trying to enjoy a parade when you are standing behind a ten-foot fence looking at it through a knothole. The only part of the parade you can see is what's right in front of you. You could enjoy it a lot more if you were above the fence. From that vantage point it would be much easier to make sense out of the parade because you could relate each segment to the beginning and end.

Like a parade, time has a beginning and an end...for us and for our planet.[5] It is framed by eternity...past and future. Looking at time from God's point of view helps us to know where our life fits in His plan.

God always has been. He is. He always will be. God is eternal. When Moses was asking God for credentials to present to Pharaoh at the time he was seeking the release of the Hebrew slaves, God told him to inform Pharaoh that the One who stands outside of time had sent him...the I Am.[6]

In the strictest use of the word, only God is eternal. Archangels and angels, seraphim and cherubim Satan and demons are everlasting, but they are not eternal. Even though they will have no end, they all had a beginning. Likewise, you and I are everlasting, but we are not eternal. We had a beginning. Only God is eternal.

The Apostle James says that there is no variableness with God...no shadow of turning.[7] The Bible tells us that He is the "same yesterday, today, and forever."[8] His presence never changes!

God is not only eternal, but He is also omnipresent. He is everywhere all the time. In reflecting on God's omniscient. David laments that there is nowhere for him to flee from God's presence. [9]

There is nothing God does not know. He is omniscient. This is why it is so foolish for us to try to hide things from God. The Bible says that "...all things are naked and opened unto His eyes..."[10]

In her kind and benevolent way a grandmother was trying to teach her grandson that God was omnipresent and omniscient without relying on words too big for a four-year-old. So she said,

"You know honey, God goes everywhere you go and sees everything you do."

"Are you sure?" the little boy asked.

"I'm sure," his grandmother reassured him.

Pressing his inquiry a little further the boy asked, "Can He see me right now?"

"Yes, he can," insisted the grandmother.

Conceding her point, the four-year-old looked through the only window in the kitchen and replied, "Well, if He can see me right now then He has to be looking through that window."

Making sense out of your life becomes much easier when you see it from an eternal perspective. From that vantage point you can fit your life into God's eternal plan. Some people seem unable to do this—unable to catch a vision of the eternal. They keep their eyes glued to the knothole in the fence of the present while ignoring the eternal. People who fail to see life from an eternal perspective have lost sight of the spectacular triumph God has saved for the end of the parade. [11]

In my own life, I have discovered an exciting plan that keeps a fresh sense of purpose and direction in my life. Daily exploration of God's loving message to humanity in the Bible, and daily visiting with God through prayer free me from the "knothole" of the present and help me maintain an eternal perspective on my daily activities.

From the Scriptures we learn that God is omnipresent. He is everywhere all the time. And, He was there before anything else was created. This is so hard to grasp.

Imagining When Nothing Existed

Try to imagine a point in eternity past when nothing existed but God. Nothing He would create had yet been made. [12] Nothing!

No other spirit beings existed. No archangels. No angels.

No seraphim. No cherubim. No matter had yet been created. No galaxies. No planets or asteroids. No solar system. No Earth. There was no sun. No moon. No seas. No sky. Nothing!

No earth creatures had yet been made. No fish. No trees. No birds. No living thing that crawled or walked. No people. Nothing except a vast, dark "void"—an enormous "nothing!"

But even when nothing was there, eternity was not without a Presence. The Bible assures us that the Creator was there.[13] God was there in eternity past!

God reminded Job that He was there to lay the foundations of the earth, to call the constellations into existence and establish the laws of the heavens.[14] No human being was there to witness it, but God was there. Job struggled to imagine what eternity must have been like when only God was there.

Imagining What God Is Like

For a moment, let's enter into that struggle with Job. What do *you* suppose eternity was like when only God was there? Try to imagine sharing that moment of creation with Him. What kind of feeling would such a moment stimulate in you? Do you wish you could have shared that moment with Him when He called the universe into existence out of nothing? Or, would you rather not have been there? Pondering your answers to questions such as these will help you get in touch with your feelings and thoughts about God.

Your Mental Picture of God

The presence of God is more attractive for those who have a healthy image of Him. Remember, no one relates to God as He actually is. Our finite minds cannot possibly comprehend God. Each of us relates to Him as we have learned to picture Him in our mind. How do you picture God in your mind? As you focus on these pictures, what feelings and thoughts begin to surface? Our feelings and thoughts about God come from our mental images of Him. The mental images you have of God play a vital role in your spiritual, emotional and social health.

Our images of God are mostly formed before our seventh year. They grow out of our relationships with our parents—particularly our father. Of course, the way you see God is also by your church life, particularly during the preschool and early elementary years. However, the home has a far greater spiritual influence on a child's life than the school. After all, our parents are our earliest authority figures. They create a presence in our minds long before we become aware of God's presence.

The way we feel and think about our parents affect the way we feel and think about every other authority figure in life—including God. Since God is so much bigger than our parents often He becomes a gigantic replica of them in our minds.

For example, if our parents are hard to please and often angry with us, then we may see God as hard to please and often angry with us. In this case, when we are old enough to read the Bible for ourselves we subconsciously focus on those Scriptures that reinforce the ways we have already learned to feel and think about God. We see Him drowning everybody in the flood, raining down fire and brimstone on people, killing all the Canaanites, and arbitrarily sending everyone to Hell who displeases Him in any way.

If these are your mental pictures of God then being there with Him in eternity past when only He was creating the universe has no appeal to you. You are likely to picture this moment as a time of ultimate fury.

If your parents were violent with each other or with you, then you may fear God will be violent with you. If your father left your mother early in your life, or was seldom involved with you, then you may feel abandoned by a God who is remote and disinterested in you.

On the other hand, if your parents were loving people, if they gave you plenty of affection and kept their approval within your reach most of the time, if you frequently saw them hug and kiss each other, then you are likely to see God as One Who loves you very much and keeps His approval within your reach.

Even though we may not have come from a religious family, somewhere between our birth and our death God confronts each of us with His Presence. Each of us choose our response to this divine moment. Some chooses to ignore Him. Others choose to discover Him. However, ultimately death will usher each of us into His Presence. When we leave this world we will step into the Presence of the One who was there before anything was called into existence.

Let the Scriptures Edit Your View of God

I often counsel people not to impose childhood memories of angry and judgmental parents onto the way they picture God. As we read all of God's Word, we can let the Scriptures lovingly describe Him for us. Doing this helps us correct any distorted images left by painful parental memories and reveals to us the God of grace.

Then, you will see Him in the Old Testament forgiving an endless line of His erring children and repeatedly winning back Israel's heart from her backsliding ways. In the New Testament you will see His fathomless love in giving His Son to die for our sins.[15]

Although the Bible pictures God as angry at sin and injustice in His world, His overriding nature is unmistakably portrayed as merciful, loving, and forgiving.[16] If you and I could have been there for that awesome moment when creation began we would have been ecstatic as God's loving, peaceful, joyful presence gave birth to creation.

Job describes creation as this kind of joyous moment.[17] David says God's presence is full of joy and pleasure.[18] When Jesus faced the darkest time of His life on Earth, He drew strength from the love He remembered enjoying with the Father before the world began.[19]

In eternity past, then, the Father, Son, and Holy Spirit celebrated a community of love, joy, and peace. They dwelt in unbroken unity. They lacked nothing. They needed nothing. Eternity was charged with their dynamic buoyant presence.

God did not need to create anything...nor was He under any obligation to create. He is sufficient in all ways. He has no needs. His rapturous presence leaves nothing to be added.

Why Did God Create?

As an omnipotent God, He knew before He created the angels that Lucifer would lead a third of the angels in a rebellion against Him. So why did He choose to create them?

When God created Adam and Eve, He commissioned them to multiply, replenish the earth, subdue it, and restore divine dominion over it, He knew they would fail. So why did He choose to create them?

Why did God choose to create any being capable of deciding to do something other than His will? Honestly, we don't know.

However, as earthly parents we may ask that same question of ourselves. When we chose to have children, didn't we know that they could choose to disobey us? Why then did we have children? They are the product of our love. So, creation is a product of God's love. And, *anything love creates is blessed with freedom.*

In this life, we will never know *why* God chose to create, but we know that He did. He didn't have to do it. But for reasons known only to Him, a loving and benevolent God chose to create and give birth to the universe. And when He did, His awesome power and His loving presence exploded throughout space.

Creation, then, is a projection of who God is. And because He is a loving and good God, everything He chose to create was good.[20] Some of Creation had the freedom to be evil, and we'll talk about that later. But at the time He created everything, everything that He created was good.

How Did God Create?

Exactly *how* God created is another mystery. However, Moses and the Apostle John make two things clear: God created everything that exists, and God's Word was involved in creation.

The Word or *Logos* was God's personal agent of creation. This is how John says it,

> *"In the beginning was the Word, and the Word was with God, and the Word was God. The same was in the beginning with God. All things were made by him; and without him was not anything made that was made."*[21]

In describing the creation of Earth, Moses simply declares, *"And God said, Let there be light: and there was light."*[22]

When Did God Create?

The most widely accepted scientific explanation is that the universe began between 18 and 20 billion years ago in a powerful explosion of a very dense, very small amount of "matter."

With one "Big Bang," that lump of matter exploded. The pieces continue to move outward. All the planetary, stellar, and other matter of the universe is moving "out" and away from all other matter.[23] Interestingly, sound and light, the same two dynamics involved in the prevailing scientific explanation of creation are central to the biblical account of creation. The sound of God's voice was the first expression of creation, and light sprang forth from that sound.[24]

Astronomers believe that today's powerful telescopes are enabling them to see over 90 percent of the way back in time toward the origin of the universe. From the information they have gathered, many now agree that the universe was launched with a big bang and that it continues to expand.[25]

However, no one knows exactly how creation happened.[26] All we can know for sure is that God, operating in His kingdom of timelessness and space, spoke the universe into existence in ways that are beyond our understanding. If we needed to know how He created the universe in order to know *Him*, He would have left us significant galactic evidence to discover this secret or clearly explained the process to us in His Word.

So, even though we don't know how He did it, we do know God expressed himself in an awesome display of creation.[27] The writer of Hebrews declares that it is "by faith" we believe God created everything that is seen out of nothing.[28] And either we believe it, or we don't. It's just that simple!

So creation sprang into being as an expression of this loving, joyful, peaceful, all-powerful One the Bible calls God. The One who is there "from everlasting to everlasting,"[29] created the universe as a projection of His Presence.

The Presence of Angels

Angels are special creations of God. They do not procreate. This is why angels are referred to as a *company*...not a race. The Bible does not tell us the number of angels; it simply says they are innumerable.[30] According to the Book of Job, angels were present when God called the universe into existence.[31]

Can you imagine what that moment must have been like for them? Suddenly, without warning a thunderous voice reverberates throughout the endless expanse of space detonating a spectacular display of lights so vast as to make the wildest fireworks show on earth look like the light of an undernourished firefly.

Why Were Angels Created?

Angels were created to reflect the presence of their Creator. They are special intermediaries, agents, and messengers of God in bringing His will to pass on earth even as they do in heaven. They are ministering spirits who carry out missions to nations and people.[32]

An angel ministered to Hagar as a single mom when she had been cast out of Abraham's household.[33] Angels went with the children of Israel as they left Egypt for the Promised Land.[34] An angel shut the lions' mouths for Daniel and an angel opened prison doors for the apostles.[35]

While on the isle of Patmos where he was exiled for his faith, John saw the angels in heaven. He was so overwhelmed by the sheer number of angels as he attempted to write what he saw, he didn't even try to count them. He simply said there were ten thousand times ten thousand and thousands of thousands.[36]

We may never know when God's angels are involved in our lives. One of the many surprises we can expect in heaven is the discovery of how often angels, perhaps thousands of them, were involved in our lives on earth. This is why God's Word encourages us . . . *"to be kind to strangers, for some who have done this have entertained angels without realizing it!"*[37]

God's company of angels is ranked and organized. The Scriptures refer to captains, princes and chief princes of the Lord's host. There are Cherubim who defend God's holiness.[39] There are Seraphim who worship and extol God's holiness.[40] There are archangels: Michael a mighty warrior[41], Gabriel a special messenger[42]. Some angels are God's vice regents who are given jurisdiction over certain parts of the universe.[43] When needed, angels can be dispatched in legions—a measurement in the Roman army at the time of Christ designating 6,000 men. Angels form the armies of the Lord, who will defeat Satan in the end.[44]

Throughout the Bible, angels appeared in public places,

spoke softly in the language of dreams, or shone brightly with God's reflected glory. Although not omniscient or omnipotent like God, angels are far wiser and stronger than any human. Their astounding power is demonstrated repeatedly throughout Scripture. For example, a single angel killed 185,000 Assyrians in one night while defending God's people.[45]

Angels are also God's messengers. The angel Gabriel stood on the altar in the temple and told Zechariah about the coming births of Christ and John the Baptist. The same angel delivered the news to Mary.[46] And he reassured Joseph that the baby Mary had conceived was Israel's Savior.[47] Angels also announced the good news of Christ's birth to the shepherds.[48]

Angels carried out special assignments during Jesus' mission on earth. They ministered to Him after His temptation. They strengthened Him at Gethsemane. They rolled the stone away from his tomb to display His victory over the grave. They were with Him in His ascension to the Father. They will accompany Him back to Earth one day in power and glory.[49] As we will discover later, some of these angels rebelled against God under the leadership of Satan, ushering in the presence of Evil.

All Matter Has Come From Spirit

What practical lessons can we learn from the biblical descriptions of the nature of God and His presence in creation, and what difference can it make in our lives?

The first and most obvious lesson to be learned is that God is a Spirit and from that Spirit all matter has come into existence.[50] He created everything that exists from nothing. He gave life to everything that lives. He has done this in ways that defy human explanation. Scientists have stumbled onto part of His secret in the "Big Bang" theory of creation, but they cannot identify *what* went "bang" in the first place or *why* it went bang. This still defies scientific explanation—it's a mystery known only to

God. The human mind lacks the capacity to imagine the power and energy released in that flashing moment of eternity. The practical lesson to be learned from this is that all matter has come from Spirit

"By faith we understand that the universe was formed at God's command, so that what is seen was not made out of what was visible."[51] God, Who is Spirit, created our material universe out of nothing. *Matter came from Spirit—not the other way around.* . . so the spiritual concerns of life should have priority over the material concerns of life.[52]

This simple observation should inspire us to observe this discipline in our lives. However, in a society as materialistic as ours, this is not an easy discipline to learn. Evil continually tempts us to substitute counterfeit material pleasures for the love, joy, and peace that only God's presence can bring to us.[53]

In His "Sermon on the Mount" Jesus tells us to seek the kingdom of God and His righteousness first. What is the kingdom of God? It is not a material kingdom. It is a kingdom of righteousness, peace, and joy in the Holy Spirit.[54] Jesus guarantees us that God will take care of our material needs if we put Him first.

Spirit Is More Powerful Than Matter

A second important lesson of life emerges from God's account of creation. Since all matter has come from spirit, spirit is more powerful than matter. No one will ever understand how matter emerged from Spirit. As we said earlier, there is no explanation for the origin of the mass of exploding material. Only by faith can we know that the Word of God created everything...out of nothing.

Since spirit is more powerful than matter, the spiritual issues of life are of greater importance than the material issues. But as Westerners, we seem to have difficulty giving priority to realities that defy rational or scientific explanation. We strongly favor giving priority to the material and the immediate rather than the spiritual and eternal. We prefer to focus on things we can touch, taste, see, smell, and hear. Our preoccupation with the "sweet here-and-now," tends to blind us to the more deeply satisfying realities of the "sweet by-and-by."

We struggle with the conflict between matter and spirit far more than people in Eastern/Asian cultures. In these cultures, where mystical religions are commonplace, people seldom see any contradiction or discontinuity between their science and the convictions of their religious belief.

On the other hand, secular scientists in Western countries are more likely to see their science as contradictory to any belief in God. They rationalize this stance by assuming that since the existence of God can't be scientifically proven, it is inconsistent with science to believe He is there. Even more dangerous, they often see science as the superior path to truth, rather than faith. In a sense, science becomes a substitute for God in their lives. They look to science for answers to the big questions of life. They place their faith in truth as defined by science rather than truth as defined by Scripture. Holding reason to be superior to faith makes it virtually impossible to experience the Presence of God.

Science should be respected as an effective way of defining truth related to the natural world. However, truth as defined by science is so tenuous and transient. A theory that is in favor today may be disproved and replaced by a very different theory tomorrow.

Many scientists are skeptical of faith and many believers are distrustful of science. Each community holds the other suspect. For many, in both camps, science and faith are like oil and water. The two simply do not mix. However, faith and science need not pre-empt each other.

Faith and True Science Are One

Ideological warfare between faith and science has not always existed. Many pioneers of the "age of science" believed that the existence of the universe could only be understood as the work of an intelligent Creator. They believed their sciences were possible because the Creator had brought into existence an ordered, predictable universe that could be gradually known by discovering the predictable scientific laws that governed it. They believed that things like gravity; earth's rotation around the sun; the moon's rotation around earth; the human body; and the life cycles of plants and animals were able to be studied and understood because they were predictable creations of an intelligent thoughtful, and orderly Creator.[55] This attitude left science with openness toward the presence and existence of God. A person could both expand his understanding of nature through science and extend his knowledge of God through faith.

More recently, the scientific community has gone to the other extreme. Instead of using faith in an intelligent God to better understand His creation, scientists place their faith only in the scientific, empirical method of discovering and defining truth. They only believe in those things that can be proven to exist. This unnecessary alienation of science from faith hinders many in the scientific community from finding a relationship with the Creator that can bring meaning and purpose to their lives.

Today, science is preoccupied with the material world and tends to support a materialistic approach to life. Consequently, both science and materialism are turning some hearts away from God.

Faith and Materialism Do Not Mix

Although faith and true science should blend together naturally, *faith and materialism do not mix*. Faith focuses on the

Maker, materialism focuses on what is made. Faith directs its search inward and upward longing to be filled with the presence of the One from whom all things have come. Materialism greedily reaches outward and downward lusting after an abundance of things.

Materialists measure their success and even their self worth in terms of money and possessions. It is not how far they have come from nothing that consumes them, but rather an acute awareness of how their possessions and financial worth compare with others.

Money and stuff become the gods of materialists. In many ways they are no different from those who worship idols and creatures of creation. They are possessed by their things rather than by the Maker of all things. Consequently, materialists use people to get things instead of using things to serve people. Paul identifies the folly of this by reminding us, "*We brought nothing into the world, and we can take nothing out.*"[56]

Whether we are rich or poor by earthly standards, this material house—this body we live in— is going back to dust when our spirit leaves it for eternity. If we have housed His loving, joyful, peaceful Presence in our body on earth, then we can look forward to celebrating that same Presence when we go to be with Him. If we have lived for God on earth, we will find ourselves in the Presence of the God of eternity.

However, as we will discuss in the following chapter, there is an evil one at large in our world. He is committed to deceiving us with fleeting pleasures and false promise of happiness. If we let him, he will deny us the joy of God's presence on earth; and banish us from God's Presence in eternity.

FOOTNOTES

[1] Grenz, Stanley J., *Theology for the Community of God* (Grand Rapdis, Mich.: William B. Erdman's Publishing Company, 1994), 72.

[2] Psalms 8:1, 3

[3] Existential questions attempt to ascribe meaning and purpose to one's existence.

[4] II Peter 3:8

[5] Hebrews 9:27; II Peter 3:8-10; Revelation 21:1

[6] Exodus 3:14

[7] James 1:17

[8] Hebrews 13:8

[9] Psalms 139:7-8

[10] Hebrews 4:13

[11] I Corinthians 15:19

[12] Genesis 1:1, John 1:1-3

[13] John 1:1

[14] Job 38:4-7; 31-33

[15] Galatians 2:19-20

[16] John 3:16,17

[17] Job 38:7

[18] Psalms 16:11

[19] John 17:24

[20] Genesis 1:1-3; John 1:1-3

[21] John 1:2, 3

[22] Genesis 1:3

[23] The World Almanac and Book of Facts 2001, World Almanac Books, Mahwah, New Jersey, 2001, p. 585.

[24] Genesis 1:3

[25] Recer, Paul. "Stargazers Pinpoint Galaxy;" Akron Beacon Journal, May 2, 1998, p.9.

[26] Ibid

[27] Psalm 8:3, 4

[28] Hebrews 11:3

[29] Psalm 90"2

[30] Hebrews 12:22

[31] Job 38:7

[32] Hebrews 1:7

[33] Genesis 16:7

[34] Exodus 23:20, 23

[35] Daniel 6:22; Acts 5:19

[36] Revelation 5:11

[37] Hebrews 13:2 (The Living Bible)

[38] Joshua 5:15; Daniel 10:13, 20-21

[39] Genesis 3:24; Exodus 25:18; I Kings 6:23-28

[40] Isaiah 6:2

[41] Jude 9; Revelation 12:7

[42] Daniel 8:15-26; 9:21-27; Luke 1:11-20; 26-35

[43] Ephesians 6:12; II Corinthians 10:4

[44] Revelation 19:14

[45] II Kings 19:35

[46] Luke 1:11-38

[47] Matthew 1:18-25

[48] Luke 2:8-18

[49] Matthew 4:11; Luke 22:43; Matthew 28:2-7; Acts 1:11; Matthew 25:31

[50] John 4:24

[51] Hebrews 11:3

[52] Matthew 6:31-34

[53] Galatians 5:22

[54] Romans 14:17

[55] Barzun, Jacques, >From Dawn to Decadence: 1500 to the Present. Harper/Collins Publishers; New York, NY; 2000, p.198

[56] I Timothy 6:7

CHAPTER THREE

HUMAN
PRESENCE

On the ceiling of the Vatican's Sistine Chapel Michelangelo's frescoes capture the awesome moments when God created Adam and Eve. The first time I saw them I was totally unprepared for the emotional impact they had on me. For several minutes I stood with my neck craned back as far as possible, my mouth agape, my spirit overwhelmed. I was speechless.

There was no human observer there to describe what actually took place, but the artist portrays angels around the figure of God, curiously staring as He made this magnificent creation, the first human being. There is a jubilant look on God's face as He extends His outstretched hand toward Adam who is sitting up, leaning forward with his hand eager to grasp the hand of God. The scene is so graphic you can almost feel the transmission of life from God's hand to Adam's as he stirs from the dust and rises to stand face to face with his Maker.

Turning my head slightly to the left, I found myself equally fascinated with the artist's amazing depiction of the creation of Eve. Adam is pictured soundly asleep in a reclining position as God brings Eve out of his side. The angels are watching in curious wonderment while God prepares this one-of-a-kind couple for their mission on earth.

For five days God had worked unceasingly to prepare the earth for human existence. He had created everything necessary to sustain human life. Then, on the sixth day He made Adam and Eve. They stood out from the rest of creation. They were unique. There was nothing on earth like them. They were the only creatures with the capacity to house God's presence on earth. God left His divine imprint on them.

Adam Was Created in Two Stages

We know very little about how God created the angels, but the Bible gives us many specific details about the creation of Adam and Eve. First, God brought Adam's body from the dust of the earth. In describing how Adam was "formed," Moses uses an interesting Hebrew word— "yatsar"— which suggests that much like a potter first has a mental picture of a vessel he wants to make and then shapes the clay, God had a pre-conceived image of Adam in His mind before He formed him from the dust of the earth.

When God had finished Adam's body it lay lifeless on the ground. Then God "breathed into his nostrils the breath of life."[1] So part of Adam was from earth, the planet he was to restore to divine dominion; and part of him was from God.

The breath of God energizing the dust of earth brought Adam to life as "a living soul," an earthen urn for housing God's presence on earth.[2] We don't know how long Adam existed before God created Eve, but we do know that this was a lonely time for him. And God said this was not good!

No other creature seemed to be a suitable companion for Adam, so God put him to sleep and created Eve from a rib He took out of Adam's side.[3] Since she was a part of Adam she shared his capacity for housing God's presence in her body.

By taking Eve from Adam's side God symbolically expressed the equality of their status. Eve was not taken from Adam's head to rule over him or from his feet to be dominated by him, but from his side to be a "joint heir" with him of the grace of life.[4] Unlike any other creatures on earth Adam and Eve were uniquely identified by God's unmistakable imprint.

They Were to Express God's Image

Adam and Eve were to grow into God's likeness by communicating with Him through their spirit/mind. They were to transform that communication into attitudes and behavior that would physically express God's likeness on earth. This transformation was to occur through their mind/brain. Notice the critical role the mind plays in this miraculous transformation of spiritual reality into physical reality.[5]

The Mind Is the Interface Between Spirit and Matter

God created the human mind to serve as the interface between the spiritual and physical worlds. Your mind links your spirit with the invisible spiritual world. Your mind also links your body with the visible physical world. The spiritual realities of your life are experienced and expressed through your mind. The physical realities of your life are experienced and expressed through your brain. Therefore, nothing spiritual can be physically expressed without involving your brain.

This is why I use the term "spirit/mind" when referring to the communication between the invisible spiritual world and our mental activities. But when speaking of the mind's role in giving physical expression to our spiritual *choices* I prefer to use the term "mind/brain." The mind has direct communication with the invisible spiritual world (spirit/mind), and indirect communication with visible physical world through our brain (mind/brain).

Your mind or spirit is in continual communication with the realities of the spiritual world and transmits those realities to your brain where they are experienced as urges, fantasies, and ideas.

Finally, your spirit, with the help of your brain, engages in a conscious struggle to determine which urges, fantasies, and ideas should be physically expressed through your body and which ones should be denied expression. As a consequence, your presence becomes defined by the attitudes and behavior finally expressed through your body as a result of this spiritual process.

Although the interaction between the spiritual (mind)

and physical (brain) world is much more complex, the process is similar to the transmission, reception, and translation of light waves and sound waves in a television. The TV, like the mind/brain, possesses the ability to translate invisible pictures and inaudible sounds into programs of visible pictures and audible sounds. However, the viewer of the TV is the one responsible for choosing which pictures and sounds are to be seen and heard. That is, the viewer has the freedom and the responsibility for choosing which programs he or she will see and hear.

Channel-surfing on the TV with the remote control is a favorite pastime for many men. Very few of us are aware that this activity reflects the state of our will at the moment. Where we pause to spend a few seconds and our eventual choice of a program are not often seen to be moral judgments . . . but they are.

When we are surfing the TV channels we are in a rapid-cycling mode of decision-making. In this frame of mind the enemy can take advantage of our semi-hypnotic state to tempt us into spiritual compromise. Every day we make hundreds of these kinds of moral judgments through a mental process that is much more subtle than our use of the remote control.

Your Mind and Your Brain Are Not the Same

Don't mistake your brain for your mind. They are not the same. After all, if your mind is simply a function of your brain, when your brain dies what happens to your mind? Does it cease to exist? Of course not! The brain serves the mind, but is distinct from it.

Without the physical organ of the brain your spirit/mind would have no way of physically expressing the unique attitudes and behaviors that form your identity. Your brain is a vitally important physical organ and you are dependent upon it for expressing your presence. But without your mind your brain is incapable of intelligent behavior. For example, the brain cannot marvel at nature. It has no sense of humor. It cannot make a decision. It is limited to such organic behaviors as tics and seizures. Your brain is the servant of your mind.

Death will destroy your brain, but your mind is a function of your spirit and is everlasting. Nevertheless, as long as we are on earth the mind and the brain are inseparable. This is why I have referred to them as the mind/brain.

As you can see, our mental activities are not simply the product of neurohormones, neurotransmitters, and receptors that enable various parts of the brain to communicate with each other. You and I consist of far more than electrical circuitry and brain waves.

God designed us to respond to and interact with both the invisible spiritual world and our visible physical environment. However, spiritual realities (both good and evil) are by far, the most powerful stimulants of our mental activities. They are the sources of many of our urges, fantasies, and ideas. Each of us is given the freedom and responsibility for choosing which of these stimuli we will express and which we will deny expression. From our choices comes our presence that leaves an imprint on others...for good or evil.

The Computer and the Programmer

Computer science gives us another useful analogy for understanding the relationship between the spiritual world, our spirit, our mind, and our brain. Think of your brain as a computer. Your body and brain are energized by oxygenated blood much like electricity powers your computer.

Without a programmer the computer is capable of doing very little on its own. It is dependent upon the programmer for its operating system, directories, file folder and files. And without a computer the programmer's self-expression is also severely limited.

You are the programmer. Remember, programmers undergo extensive training for expressing themselves through computers. The spiritual realities to which we choose to expose ourselves continually—God or Satan—are informing, educating, and training our spirits to physically express their presence. Although this process is volitional, we are often blind to it.[6]

We do not learn how to physically express good and evil by accident. We are trained by instruction, example, association, and experience. This training may be formal or informal, intentional or unintentional, conscious or unconscious, but, in any event we are willing learners.

We Were Created to Serve a Higher Power

The Westminster Confession states, "The chief end of man is to glorify God and to enjoy Him forever."[7] However, because of Adam's fall we are predisposed to serve God's enemy...Satan.

Jesus reminds us that, *"No man can serve two masters."*[8] This statement clearly says that every person will serve some master. Paul amplifies the role of the will in determining which master you and I choose to serve. *"Don't you know that when you offer yourselves to someone to obey him as slaves, you are slaves to the one whom you obey—whether you are slaves to sin, which leads to death, or to obedience, which leads to righteousness."*[9]

Your will determines who is in control of your spirit.[10] The one who controls your spirit controls your mind. Your mind controls your brain. So, in much the same way that the computer provides a means for the programmer to express himself, your mind/brain gives your spirit/mind a means of physical expression. The higher power we are choosing to serve at any given moment is revealed through our conversation, attitudes and behavior resulting from this process.[11]

Created to Communicate

God had verbal communication with Adam.[12] However, their communication was not limited to words. God impacted Adam's spirit/mind with urges, fantasies, and ideas. And, Adam, through his mind/brain, obediently gave them physical expression. So, urges, fantasies, and ideas that originated from God became physically expressed on earth through Adam's body. This is the purpose of the human body...to give physical expression to God's presence on earth.

Human beings are the only creatures on earth capable of translating these kinds of spiritual impressions into physical expressions. The bodies of Adam and Eve were made for the Lord.[13] Their highest joy came from exposing their spirits to His Presence and giving physical expression to His presence on earth through the urges, fantasies, and ideas He stimulated in their spirit/mind.

Language Is Unique to Humans

Adam and Eve were endowed with the ability to think and speak in elaborate symbols that represent people, places, things, and ideas. *Language* is another distinguishing characteristic that sets the human race apart from all other creatures on earth.

Once a human infant begins to talk, mental abilities grow at a pace that leave all other creatures far behind. As long as the brain is normal the dullest human infant is immeasurably brighter than the most intelligent ape. The distinction between human beings and apes is too great to be characterized as a missing *link*...it is a missing *touch*, the *imprint* of the Creator!

The origin of this unmistakable *imprint* of God defies scientific explanation. Evolutionists have not been able to account for the origin of human language. It is a gift from the heart of God so that we might be able to speak to Him and hear His voice...and communicate with others the same way.

Adam's Creative Intelligence

From the moment Adam took his first breath, he had a God-given ability to communicate with himself—to think and reason and express feelings—and to communicate with God. This ability is very important to our spiritual and emotional health.

God gave Adam amazing creative ability. He helped Adam discover this by bringing all the animals and birds to him and asking him to name them. Adam so accurately described each species that God called the creatures what Adam said they were.[14]

God wants us to discover new and creative dimensions of thought He makes available exclusively to us, His children. He wants to give us creative ways to approach the decision-making, problem-solving challenges of life that we face everyday at home and work. In the following chapters I will give some practical ways for getting in touch with these.

When God acquainted Adam with the Garden of Eden he introduced him to the *"tree of life."* He let Adam know that he could have free access to its *life-giving, sustaining fruit.* He also showed him the "tree of the knowledge of good and evil" and warned him of the eternal consequences of eating that fruit.[15] With that one exception, Adam had permission to eat of all Eden's tasty vegetation.

A Loving God Gave His Creatures Freedom

By introducing Adam to the tree of life and the tree of the knowledge of good and evil God provided him the same freedom he had already given the angels. Adam could choose to obey God or he could choose to disobey Him.

God gave Adam the freedom and the responsibility for choosing which of the urges, fantasies, and ideas stimulated in his spirit/mind he would express. Originally, the result was to be the physical expression of God's presence on earth. Adam, through his attitudes and behavior, was to live out the will of God. The likeness of God was to be projected throughout the earth by the *invisible imprint* of Adam's presence.

However, through this same process that enabled Adam to leave a divine *imprint* on earth also enabled him to become the physical expression of God's enemy. So, through his free and deliberate choices Adam was given the challenge of determining the moral nature of his presence.

How Does the Human Body Express God's Presence?

What is the process by which this transformation takes place? If we can understand this process more clearly we should be able to be more consciously involved in it and exercise greater initiative in facilitating it.

Every person has intelligence, emotion, and will. This distinguishes us from other creatures. All three of these are essential to becoming a fully functional human being. These three components relate to each other in intricate and complex ways. The will determines the unique blend of emotion and intelligence which defines our personality.

Undisciplined emotions can hurl us onto the rocks of personal disaster. Our local newspaper's front-page stories remind us of this every day. On the other hand, undisciplined intelligence can preoccupy us with fascinating details on the roadmap of life that have nothing to do with our trip. It can lead us on a dull, drab, passionless journey to a colorless country of empty dreams.

However, if we are healthy our will is strong enough to set limits on our emotions and give direction to our intelligence. This enables us to enjoy a colorful and meaningful life.

Other beings in the spirit world share these three aspects of personhood. For example, God has intelligence, emotion and will...and so does Satan. Having these things in common become the basis for our communicating with other human beings as well as with God and Satan.

God designed our spirit/mind capable of interacting with other spirit beings. Remember, our spirit/mind is the interface between the spiritual and physical worlds. It is where these two worlds meet in us. God and Satan communicate with us by impacting our spirit/mind, with urges, fantasies, and ideas at lightning-like speeds impossible for us to measure. Our spirit/mind uses our intelligence, emotions, and will to determine which of these urges, fantasies, and ideas to transmit and entertain in the brain and which ones to dismiss. In the brain these become evil's temptations or opportunities for doing God's will.

Once these powerful spiritual stimulants begin vying for expression the conflict is joined among our emotions, intelligence, and will. Even though our fallen nature biases us toward the options evil presents to us, we are not helpless in determining what we will do. A loving God provides discernment for determining the spiritual origin of these stimuli and grace that gives us the freedom to choose which of them we will obey. He is always there to give us the power to resist sin's destructive options and to express His creative choices.[16]

However, He will not impose Himself on us. If we will to resist temptation, He provides a way to escape. If we prefer the temptation He gives us the freedom of choice and allows us to suffer the consequences. This is the only way many of us acquire the judgment we need to make wiser choices in the future.

Everyone Wages This Battle Between Good and Evil

From this extremely complex relationship between the spirit/mind and the mind/brain and our own instincts to survive comes a torrent of urges, fantasies, and ideas bombarding our mind/brain with lightning-like speeds. When Satan dominates this process he dangles short-term pleasures in front of us, blinds our minds, and goads us into impulsive decisions with us giving little consideration to what their long-term consequences will be. [17] The Apostle Paul accurately describes this spiritual struggle and the wretched way we feel about ourselves when we lose it. But he also assures us that God has provided the resources for you and me to win it.[18]

Jesus Shows Us the Way to Victory

Jesus was not exempt from this kind of spiritual/mental conflict. He was tempted in every way just like you and I are,[19] and in His wilderness temptation He models for us the way to conquer our urges, fantasies, and ideas when we are tempted.[20]

I can't imagine how hungry Jesus must have been after fasting forty days and nights. Once I fasted for just seven days and I thought I was starving. How tempting it must have been for Jesus when Satan suggested the *idea* that He didn't need to suffer from hunger; as the Son of God He could turn stones into bread.

Jesus did not deny His hunger, but He knew where this *idea* came from and He rejected it. As tempting as it may have been, Jesus refused to let His body dominate His Spirit. Instead, He demonstrated the power of Scripture to help us resist temptation. "It is written," He said, *"Man shall not live by bread alone, but by every word that proceeds out of the mouth of God."*[21]

Then the devil took Jesus to Jerusalem and sat Him on a high point of the temple tempting Him with an *urge* to jump. Satan taunted Jesus by suggesting that since He was the Son of God, angels would be dispatched to snatch Him up before He could hit the ground. Again, Jesus disarms this tempting *urge* with Scripture. "You shall not tempt the Lord your God."[22]

Finally, the devil appealed to Jesus' *fantasy*. He took Him to the top of a very high mountain. From that vantage point it seemed like the whole world was spread before Him. "Fall down and worship me," Satan said, "and I will give you all the kingdoms of this world." Jesus knew that between that moment of temptation and His millennial "Hallelujah Chorus" lay the agonizing death of Calvary.[23] Yet, without a moment's hesitation He again drew from Scripture the power to put His enemy to flight. *"You shall worship the Lord your God, and Him only shall you serve."*[24]

In His Spirit/mind Jesus engaged Satan in spiritual warfare. He successfully resisted Satan's *idea* (turning the stones into bread), Satan's *urge* (jumping off the temple), and Satan's fantasy (a way to gain the kingdoms of this world without Calvary). Then the devil left Jesus and angels came and ministered to Him.[25]

Just as He recognized and disarmed Satan's *urges, fantasies, and ideas* in His own wilderness of temptation, Jesus will help us do the same. If we are willing to learn, He will teach us how to discern the spiritual origins of our *urges, fantasies, and ideas*; clarify our options; anticipate their consequences, and make decisions that enable us to escape the temptation.[26]

In spite of our tendency toward evil and Satan's mark on our fallen nature, God's only begotten Son and Second Adam can transform our lives into creative human expressions of His life. However, this kind of divine intervention in our lives is not magical. It does not occur without our disciplined involvement. As we will find in the next chapter, the same formidable foe who was bold enough to try to mar the perfect reflection of the Father in the life of the Son is poised to destroy the image of the Son in you and in me.

FOOTNOTES

[1] Genesis 2:7
[2] I Corinthians 15:47; I Thessalonians 5:23
[3] Genesis 2:21
[4] I Peter 3:8
[5] Romans 12:1-2
[6] Geremiah 17:9-10
[7] Thiessen, Henry C. Lectures in Systematic Theology, Wm. B.Eerdman's Pub. Co., Grand Rapids Michigan, 1949, p. 432
[8] Matthew 6:24
[9] Romans 6:16
[10] Proverbs 16:32
[11] Matthew 12:34-37
[12] Genesis 3:8-13
[13] I Corinthians 6:13
[14] Genesis 2:19-20
[15] Genesis 2:16-17
[16] I Corinthians 10:13; John 10:10
[17] II Corinthians 4:4
[18] Romans 6:11-:;:25
[19] Hebrews 4:15
[20] Matthew 4:1-11
[21] Deuteronomy 8:3
[22] Deuteronomy 6:16
[23] Revelation 20:4
[24] Exodus 34:14
[25] Matthew 4:11
[26] Hebrews 2:18

CHAPTER FOUR

THE

PRESENCE

OF

EVIL

"A creature revolting against a Creator is revolting against the source of his own powers—including even his power to revolt...it is like the scent of a flower trying to destroy the flower." C. S. Lewis

Like most of you, I sat with my eyes riveted to the television. I was stunned. I couldn't believe my eyes and ears. What I was seeing and hearing was outrageous... surreal. The regular morning television programs had been interrupted with live pictures of a raging inferno belching out billows of smoke and walls of fire from the upper floors of one of the twin towers of the World Trade Center in New York City. I am sure you felt it too.

Together we watched with horror as bedlam erupted. Thousands of people making their way down the seemingly endless flights of stairs, streaming out onto the streets surrounding the towers of the World Trade Center. We watched the brave firemen and policemen flooding the scene rushing into the buildings to evacuate people. Never in our wildest dreams could we have imagined anything like this—a jumbo jet ramming one of the World Trade Towers.

Commentators, trying to overcome their own sense of shock, struggled for words to describe what we were witnessing. Then, in less than an hour more of the unbelievable happened. I wanted to believe I was seeing a television re-enactment of the first tragedy. But with the whole world confirming what we were seeing there was no way denying it...a second jumbo jet was cutting its way through the other twin tower about twenty-five floors from the top.

By this time, more firemen and policemen than any of us had ever seen at one place were bravely rushing into both buildings desperately trying to rescue as many people as possible from these flaming infernos. Hundreds of them gave their lives in their desperate efforts to save the victims. Only God knows how many people owe their survival to these brave men and women... modern heroes that we will never forget.

In the upper floors of both buildings hundreds of people were trapped, forced to choose between two dreadful ways of dying—living cremation or a suicidal leap. People on site and in the television audience gasped with horror as many of these victims hurled themselves from the windows opting for a less painful and more sudden death.

What happened next, nobody but the brave firemen anticipated. We all watched in horror as the first tower began to collapse as though it were being imploded. The world watched in real time as tons of steel, concrete, and other debris began cascading down onto the streets below. A nation's collective heart began to race as pandemonium erupted and hundreds of people wildly ran wherever they could find space, trying to flee from the flying debris and thick clouds of dust thunderously pursuing them through the concrete canyons of lower Manhattan.

It seemed the nightmare would not end as minutes later we all watched the second tower collapse. As the catastrophe unfolded before the world, news came of the third plane crashing into the Pentagon. Seeing this monument to America's military might ripped open by an American commercial jetliner turned into a giant incendiary bomb by a crazed suicidal enemy severely deepened the gash of vulnerability sweeping across our collective consciousness.

The story kept unfolding. Stories of heros and horror began to come in about the fourth hijacked jet crashing in Western Pennsylvania.

Then the tragic individual stories of families, policemen, firemen that played out in front of us day after day made September 11, 2001 another "day of infamy" we shall never forget in the history of America.

I am old enough to have vivid memories of President Franklin Roosevelt giving his famous "day of infamy" speech in

1941. However, the vulnerability I felt as an American on September 11, 2001 far exceeded what I remember from the bombing of Pearl Harbor.

I am sure you felt as I did, listening to the intimate final words of many victims who phoned their loved ones to say, "Good-bye, I will always love you," bringing tears to our eyes. It was almost like we were encroaching on holy ground, yet these heartbreaking farewells unmasked what took place that day as the evil that it is.

We do not live in a morally neutral environment. Our world is evil. What happened at the World Trade Center is an unforgettable reminder of this. If the deaths of these thousands of people can awaken us to the deadly threat evil poses for the future of our society then some good will have come from this senseless tragedy. After all, the future of our society and the civilized world is at stake.

The same mastermind of evil responsible for this destructive genius of terrorism is making obvious inroads on the moral battlefield of our families where the future of our youth is at stake. Every day tens of thousands of our teenagers crowd this nation's juvenile correctional facilities, thousands run away from home and hundreds contract sexually transmitted diseases. Homicide is now the third highest cause of death for young people between 12 and 25; and, suicide is the second. Drug abuse continues to destroy tens of thousands of our youth every year . . . and new forms of illegal drugs arrive on our streets with alarming regularity.

Every day in our country thousands of teenage girls get pregnant. Over a thousand of them give birth to a baby. Most of them will be incapable of raising her baby to be a responsible adult. Over a thousand other teenage girls will get abortions and hundreds of them will miscarry a child. And, there is a teenage boy involved in every one of these sad situations. That life should become so painful, to so many, so soon...is evil!

Statistics alone can't reflect the pain and emptiness in the eyes of someone's daughter or son . . . brother or sister . . . caught up by and sold out to their urges, fantasies, and ideas. These young people and their families will be seriously scarred for years if not decades by destructive decisions made impulsively in response to environments similar to that described in the beginning of this chapter. How can anyone doubt the reality of evil?

Behind the faces of evil in our society is a single diabolical mind bent on stealing, killing, and destroying anything that is good and beautiful about life.[2] The Bible likens this rampant foraging of Evil to *"a roaring Lion, roaming to and fro about the earth, seeking whom he may devour."*[3]

God never intended this destructive contagion conceived in the heart of an arrogant angel to plague His celestial family nor to inflict its damage on the human race. However, when a God of love chooses to create, He gives His creatures freedom. Angels and human beings have the power of choice. They can choose to obey or disobey, to create or destroy, to live or die.

Evil Is Everlasting, But Not Eternal!

The presence of evil has been around for a long time, but it isn't eternal. Only God is eternal. He is the only One without a beginning or an end. Although there will be no end of evil, there was a beginning. It had its roots in a fallen angel named Lucifer. He was created perfect and stayed that way until he gave birth to sin.[4] The destructive force spawned in the heart of Lucifer infected heaven before it invaded earth. Remember, Evil began in heaven and spread to earth. It began among angels before it infected the human race.

Angels Turned Evil and War Broke Out in the Heavens

No one knows how long the world of angels celebrated the unbroken joy and peace of God's loving presence or how long they resisted Lucifer's efforts to enlist them in his diabolical effort to usurp God's throne. However, Lucifer's moment came and he seized it. The most powerful of all angels launched his rebellion against God. Paul seems to believe that Isaiah and Ezekiel eloquently capture that terrible moment in their prophecies against Babylon and Tyre.[5]

In prophesying against the King of Babylon Isaiah tells how Lucifer, whose name means "Son of the Morning," arrogantly boasted that he would exalt *his* throne—including our planet Earth—above the throne of God. This unique and powerful spirit being, created "perfect in all his ways," *willfully and deliberately* chose to challenge his Creator's authority.[6] He made a calculated attempt to overthrow his Creator by exalting his throne above the throne of God and assuming authority over the universe.

According to the book of Revelation, Lucifer was so powerful and persuasive he swept a third of the angels up in his coup against God.[7] He convinced them that he would one day sit on God's throne and they would share in his glory if they followed him. Those angels gambled their eternal future on his success. The prize at stake in this battle was control of the universe.

However, the Creator refused to allow His beautiful and delicately balanced creation to be threatened by a maverick and self-willed spirit. All-out war erupted in the heavens.[8]

Lucifer Was Cast Out of heaven

Immediately, God moved to clear up any doubt about who was in control of creation. He was—and He would remain in control. Lucifer's rebellion was squelched at its inception. He and those angels who were foolish enough to follow him were cast out of heaven. Jesus told His disciples that He witnessed this unprecedented moment when God dealt with Satan.[9] Both Peter and Jude make reference to the fact that some of the angels who chose to follow Satan were subsequently incarcerated in everlasting chains awaiting their judgment.[10]

In this very moment when Lucifer made his move, hell was created for him and his angels.[11] The two-thirds of the angels who are still true to God saw clearly the consequences they escaped by refusing to be deceived into following Lucifer. This was a loving God's way of immediately rewarding them for their loyalty and reminding them of their fate if they chose a similar course in the future.

After all, there is no Biblical reason to believe that the angels who did not choose to follow Lucifer in his rebellion against God no longer have the capacity to fall. They continue to have the same freedom to choose as the fallen angels exercised in joining with Satan in his rebellion.

Since they were cast out of heaven, Satan and those spirit beings allied with him continue to be at war with God and His angels. Some people believe these "fallen angels" became "demons" who also have a "presence" here on earth.

Those angels who allied themselves with Satan reflect his presence and are *just as committed* to spreading this contagion of evil as the unfallen angels are to reflecting God's loving, peaceful presence throughout the earth. The angels who have remained faithful to God continue to worship Him and carry out His assignments throughout the universe.

Satan cannot defeat the Church or destroy the universe, but he still roams the Earth like a wounded dragon, planting evil urges, fantasies, and ideas in the hearts of men and women, always *"...seeking whom he may devour."* [12]

There is coming a time when Evil (also known as Satan and Lucifer) no longer will be free. God will cast him into hell forever.[13] Until then, he roams the earth and soars the heavens wreaking as much havoc as possible in the lives of people. He is a deceiver, "the Father of lies," yet sometimes poses as an "Angel of light."[14] This is why he can be so convincing. If he is crafty enough to deceive one-third of the angels with all of their wisdom, power, and knowledge, he is indeed clever enough to deceive you and me. Often he seeks to damage and destroy our faith by blaming on God tragedies that clearly bear his invisible imprint.

The Bible does not answer all of our questions about evil, but one thing is clear: Sin had its origin in heaven...not on earth. It was conceived in the prideful heart of Lucifer and born among the angels long before it was transmitted to Adam, Eve, and the human race.

Evil Enters the Human Race

The ugly imprint of Evil can be found all over our planet. I see it every time I have to drive past the sleazy pornographic districts around our nation's airports. Like the tentacles of a deadly cancer, pornography and the sex business take advantage of a man's sex drive and gradually destroy his capacity for tenderness and intimacy and leaves his heart full of lustful longings that drive him far from home.

And . . . I feel evil every time I allow myself to think of the hundreds of thousands of unborn babies we kill every year simply because their birth would embarrass or inconvenience us.

In my travels, I have seen shocking displays of diabolical Evil that have plagued humanity for centuries. When I stood amid the ruins of the Aztec pyramids near Mexico City I felt an evil presence. I tried to imagine the many times each year when huge throngs of Aztecs crammed into that place for pagan worship. The priests incited the crowds into ecstatic frenzies. The chanting and the drums sent people spiraling into escalating levels of emotion that would not begin to subside until twenty-four human sacrifices had been bound, placed on pyres of wood and set afire after their hearts had been ripped out. As smoke from these burnt offerings ascended the noise level would reach new peaks and finally begin to subside, as the bloodthirsty gods of the Aztecs had been satisfied one more time.

I felt another kind of evil when I stood in the ruins of Corinth and gazed up at the acropolis still standing in silent testimony of the grip the devil once had on that place. Every year, the men of Corinth would trudge their way up that hill spurred on by their lustful fantasies of the pleasure awaiting them in the arms of temple prostitutes.

Standing in the Holocaust Museum at Jerusalem reflecting on the Nazi's deliberate efforts to destroy the Jewish people I became overwhelmingly aware of another kind of evil.

I felt still another kind of evil in Kuala Lumpur, Malaysia, when a converted drug lord drove us through a drug-infested area that blights that beautiful city. There my wife and I saw scores of emaciated drug addicts slowly dying while still indulging their habits.

Satan and Evil Are Real

On all these scenes one can see the invisible imprint of Satan. He is not a mythological figure. He is a real being whose presence exudes destruction and death. Sin is not a myth. It is a power that has plagued the human mind with destructive urges, fantasies, and ideas ever since the fall of Adam and Eve.

Adam and Eve were created *"in the image of God"* and clothed with His glory.[15] These qualities are not attributed to any other created being. Only we human beings are created "in the image of God." Satan is dedicated to eradicating "the image of God" from the earth. He wants nothing left on the planet that bears a divine imprint. His mission is to wipe out "the image of God" in people and to leave in its place the imprint of his own evil presence.

Of course, Satan is fighting a losing battle, but he is determined to take as many people as possible down to defeat with him. Nevertheless, from that earliest moment of human disobedience, our loving God promised to send a Savior under whose foot the head of Satan would be bruised.[16]

Satan's Ingenious Attack

Satan knew what the creation of Adam and Eve was all about. He knew that God was determined to depose him, isolate him, and confine him and all his followers to hell.[17] Just as the plague of his evil virus of rebellion had contaminated one-third of the angels, Satan was determined to infect the whole human race with an invisible power far more deadly than anthrax spores. He began with Eve.

Here's what made Eve's temptation so irresistible. First, the fruit appealed to her desire for food. Hunger is the strongest of human drives...stronger even than the desire for sex. Second, the fruit was pleasant to the eye. It looked good. Lust begins with a look...and soon her eye lusted for it.

Third, Satan said it would make her wise like God. This appealed to Eve's pride. These three qualities characterize all human temptation: the lust of the flesh, the lust of the eye, and the pride of life.[18]

Satan specializes in lies characterized by half-truths. They are far more effective than obvious lies because they sound so convincing! For example, he assured Eve that if she ate of the tree she would be able to know the difference between good and evil. This was true. The half of the truth he did *not* tell her was that although she would be able to *know good* she would be unable to *do* it. Nor did he tell her she would *know evil*—and be *unable to refrain from doing it.*

The Definition of Sin

What is the process by which sin invades my life and expresses itself in me? How can I identify sin before I express it? An answer to these questions requires an operational definition of sin. Here is mine: "*Sin is an invisible power that comes from Satan. Its impact on the mind is to stimulate the brain to think in terms of urges, fantasies, and ideas that detract from and destroy one's divine potential.*"

Satan toyed with Eve's *fantasies* of being like God. He flirted with her *urge* to eat the fruit he made so attractive to her. He teased her with *ideas* of unlimited freedom—even the freedom to disobey God, but he carefully hid the consequences from her. He confidently reassured Eve, *"You will not surely die."*[19] She believed his lie and the rest is human history.

Notice, often he comes as an angel of light.[20] He gains his entrance through the decision-making, problem-solving activities of our mind where he stimulates urges, fantasies, and ideas that detract from and destroy our divine potential. Then, he leaves us to choose our own poison.

Eve offered Adam a piece of the fruit. Perhaps she seemed wiser or stronger to him because of her newly acquired knowledge. We'll never know—but we know that he ate the fruit. Like Eve, he didn't have to, but he did. The same Satan who had stimulated powerful urges, fantasies, and ideas into Eve's mental processes was now focused on Adam.

Had Adam chosen to turn from Eve's temptation surely God would have found a way to spare him her fate. This is in no way an attempt to vilify Eve. It is simply fixing Adam's indictment. It was Adam who chose to follow Eve rather than God. It was Adam's disobedience, not Eve's that tore the human family away from God and allied us by nature with Satan in the war for control of earth. Perhaps the deliberate nature of Adam's disobedience is still reflected in the man's being more resistant to spiritual vulnerability than the woman.

Adam did not see that God's limits were set for His protection. He was unwilling to submit himself to God's wisdom and will for his life. He did not believe that his true choice was either to be a loving servant of God (good) or a slave to Satan (evil). He took a chance on having other options.

With the advantage that comes to all who look back on other people's mistaken judgments, we like to think we would have been wiser than Adam. As the saying goes, "hindsight is twenty-twenty." Up against Satan, the chances are that our behavior wouldn't have been any different from Adam's. In our own strength, not one among us is a match for this wily and powerful enemy.

Satan deceived Adam into believing that God's restriction had put him in bondage and that disobeying God could make him totally free. Ever since, human beings have tended to feel that they are not free unless they are free to do the forbidden.

Human beings were not created to be free of any restraint. They were created to house the presence of God on Earth and freely love Him. Total freedom is an illusion Satan uses to destroy people.

Evil *Is* Powerful . . . and It *Is* at Work in Our World

I don't want to aggrandize the power of Satan, but I do want to respect it. He can be so convincing that he would deceive the very elect of God if it were possible.[21] We cannot face him in our own strength.

Jude says that when the warrior archangel Michael was contending with Satan for the body of Moses he was overpowered. This gives us some idea of what a powerful enemy Lucifer is. Even the archangel Michael was no match for Lucifer.

We Have a Sin Problem

Lucifer left the human family with a sin problem. The destructive urges, fantasies, and ideas the human mind entertains come from the Destroyer[22]. We are a self-destructive race, but we are too blind and rebellious to admit it. Solomon says, *"There is a way that seems right to a man, but in the end it leads to death."*[23]

We keep denying this. Evolutionists say there is nothing wrong with the human race that time cannot fix. Eugenic experts say there is nothing wrong with the human race that better breeding cannot fix. Educators say there is nothing wrong with the human race that more knowledge and better learning cannot fix. Time, better breeding, or education can never fix what ails the human race.

The truth is you and I have a sin problem! This is what the Bible says is wrong with the human race.[24] We are tuned into the wrong sources of urges, fantasies, and ideas. Evil's presence controls far too many human minds and spirits.

The character of a nation's adults is reflected in the choices and character of its youth. Poor choices made in youth create scars we carry for the rest of our lives. Even when God forgives us and heals the hurts of our past we still must live with the consequences of Evil's earlier presence in our lives. The impulsive and rebellious decisions we made when we were under the rule of sin still take their toll on us. We have to live out the consequences of our choices.[25]

We Are Responsible for Our Choices

I never will forget the day I saw Christine for the first time. She was calloused and hard. She had been battered and bruised by life. She looked thirty-five, but she was only nineteen. Evil had stolen her innocence and youth and in their place left its ugly undeniable *imprint*. This was her story.

Like many adolescents, Christine had found her parents "totally out of it" and unbearable—particularly her mother. Prodded by peer pressure and spurred on by rebellion, she defied any restraints her parents attempted to place on who she could have as friends, where she could go, what she could do, and when she should be home.

When her school grades plummeted from A's to F's, Christine simply refused to go back. After all, she would soon be sixteen, and in her state sixteen-year-olds are allowed to drop out of school if that is what they want to do. She did, and got a part-time job.

Driven by anger and determined to get away from home, Christine secretly began saving her money for a one-way bus ticket to New York City. Even though she had never been there, she was convinced this was where her distorted dreams could come true. She never once thought it could be the nightmare it turned out to be.

She didn't even tell her closest friends about her plan. Once she had enough money she waited for the opportunity to run away.

Christine told me how exciting it was when she finally made her break. As she boarded the bus, her imagination went wild thinking about the unrestrained freedom awaiting her in the Big Apple. Nobody there would tell her what she could or couldn't do. Nobody there would look down on her friends. And, nobody would tell her when she had to be home at night. For the first time in her life she would be totally free.

What she found when she got there was drastically different from what she expected. As the driver slowly wound his way through inner-city neighborhoods surrounding the bus terminal, Christine recalled how she was suddenly seized by tremendous fear and anxiety. As she stepped away from the security of that bus and its uniformed driver, she felt lost and alone.

Except for a couple of nights at church camp, Christine had never been away from home. She had no idea about what kind of world she was about to enter. New York is immense and overwhelming to anyone who sees it for the first time—and especially for a small-town girl.

In the major cities of our nation there is no shortage of predators waiting to take advantage of runaways like Christine. Alone there in the swirling activity of the bus terminal, her bewilderment was obvious to anyone who might be watching. The seductive traps of the enemy were baited and waiting to snare their unwary prey.

Christine didn't know one person in New York City. Her

money was limited. She had no job. She didn't even know where she was going to spend the first night. All of a sudden these facts overwhelmed her with fear, although when she had been planning her escape, they didn't seem important at all.

The "Friendly Face" of Evil

As Christine awkwardly wandered through the bus terminal, a tall good-looking man approached her and offered his assistance. He soon learned what he had expected. She had no job, no place to stay. So he offered her a place to stay for the night and promised to help her look for a job the next day. This man would leave his evil imprint on Christine's life

His manner was so disarming that before she knew it she was in his car. They were on their way to his lavish apartment. As Christine entered she was speechless. She had never seen anything like it.

The man carried her suitcase into a bedroom twice as large and much more elegantly furnished than anything her parents had ever been able to provide for her. She found herself surrounded by the very best of everything. Even though it was evident that other young women were living in the apartment, Christine naively believed they were a family.

As soon as he had put her suitcase in the bedroom and shown her around the apartment, they got back into his car and left for one of New York's most popular restaurants. At least, that's what he told her.

Christine began to wonder why this man was being so generous and while they were eating, she asked him. He told her he had grown daughters of his own. He was trying to treat her the way he would want someone to treat his daughters if they had chosen to run away from home and were alone and scared in a big city.

Christine felt that what was happening to her was too good to be true . . . and it was. But, in her twisted thinking she believed that even though she was choosing to rebel against God and her parents, God had sent this "kind" man to look out for her. How deceptive the "friendly face" of evil can be!

Satan doesn't show his deadly fangs until he has already sunk them so far into your soul that he thinks he has you forever. He approaches you in a fashionable business suit and tie or designer jeans and a custom shirt. He doesn't come at you in a red costume with horns and a tail with a pitchfork in his hands.

You're probably thinking some of the same things that went through my mind as Christine's sad story unfolded in my office that day. If this man was so concerned about her, why didn't he try to persuade her to contact her parents? Isn't that what he would have expected another parent to do if they had found his daughter in similar circumstances? However, Christine never even thought about questioning his motives. This is how deceptive evil can be.

That first night, she settled into a large, clean, comfortable bed and drew the covers up around her face to go to sleep, never dreaming she was being lured into a life of drugs and prostitution. However, she did recall feeling strange the next day when she discovered she was sharing this luxury apartment with five other girls who were a little older than she was. This was not a family . . . and she knew it!

For the first week or so, the oldest girl befriended her and educated her about her body. She taught her how to wear her clothes and told her how easy it would be for her to earn a good living in the city. She persuaded Christine to "party" with the other girls in the apartment—something that soon became a nightly habit. Within a month, Christine was hooked on drugs and totally under the control of the pimp who had posed as a Good Samaritan that first afternoon when she was alone and afraid at the bus station.

As she recalled the three sordid years of her life she spent with him, she had no idea how many men she had been with. She had simply done whatever he . . . and they had told her to do. Then, she dutifully brought him the money his clients paid for her sexual services.

Before long, she began to realize that he was not providing her and the other girls with much of anything. Instead, he was using the income from their bodies to pay for his posh Manhattan apartment, buy his designer clothes, and provide his luxury car. But by this time, Christine was too hooked on drugs to do anything about it. . .and too embarrassed to call her parents.

For three years, Christine's parents had heard nothing from her, but her mother refused to believe she was dead. She continued to pray.

By this time, Christine was desperate to find a way out of the destructive life she had chosen for herself. One day when Christine and some of the other girls went to get some things at a supermarket she found a payphone and called home. Her father answered. The conversation was brief. She wanted out of the life she was in. Christine wanted to come home.

After some hesitation, she finally told her father exactly where in New York she was. At his insistence, she agreed to go to the nearest police officer and ask for protective custody. She was afraid the officer would arrest her for prostitution, but her father assured her that this was the best thing she could do, even if she was arrested.

Her father told her to tell the police officer that she ran away from home when she was 16 and now she wanted out of the life she was in. He told her to let the officer know she had called her Dad to come and get her—and he was on his way. Christine was so desperate to escape from her life of drugs and prostitution she did exactly what her father told her to do. She went straight to the nearest police officer and told him her story.

Of course, the officer had heard many stories like Christine's, but for some reason he agreed to call her father to check it out. Her Dad assured the officer he would be on the next plane to New York, so the officer told him where Christine would be when he arrived.

As soon as her father landed in New York City he took a cab to where Christine was being held. When the two of them saw each other they broke into tears and began to celebrate a long awaited reunion.

At first, her dad wanted to press charges against the man who violated his daughter. He wanted to see the man get what was coming to him, but when he learned the kind of grueling questions his daughter would have to face on the witness stand if the case came to trial, he couldn't bring himself to impose such a humiliating experience on his daughter.

He chose instead to take her home to the people who really loved her and would try to help her put her life back together. During the flight home, Christine and her dad talked more than they had in years and began mending a lot of family fences.

Satan Is a "Sore Loser"

When her pimp discovered Christine was gone, he used his contacts to track her down. Within a few days after she was home, she got a telephone call from him. He wanted to remind her of all that he had invested in her. He threatened to hunt her down and harm her if she didn't repay him. Christine was terrified. She knew the man had connections. So, her father took the next call and reminded him of the criminal charges he could face because of Christine's age at the time he abducted her. They never heard from him again.

Why Do We Make Such Destructive Choices?

Comedians have gotten a lot of mileage out of the lame excuse, "The devil made me do it." No, the devil didn't make Christine do what she did. He only presented the urges, the fantasies, and the ideas. Christine had a will of her own and the freedom to say, "No." She made the choices herself. She was responsible for her misery. No one else made those choices for her.

When temptations like this come our way they are never our only options. There are always other options...and wiser ones. But to find them we have to be looking for them.[26] At the time, Christine wasn't.

However, once she called her father Christine began to look for and find wiser options for her future. With God's help, she eventually broke free from her past. It took several months of gut-wrenching therapy, but Christine made it!

She found a healthy church to attend. She decided to get her High School equivalency diploma and go to college. She became an elementary school teacher. Eventually, she married a young man from her church. She and her husband are the proud parents of two sons and a daughter.

Evil Takes Its Toll, But Grace Prevails

Once we choose to express it, evil always takes its toll. Christine's youth and innocence were sacrificed on the altar of her defiance and rebellion. There was no way for her to retrieve them.

God forgave her for fostering the rebellious nature that drove her from her parents and away from home. He forgave her for prostituting herself during those three years. However, forgiveness does not cancel the laws of the harvest. These laws and their consequences are as inevitable in the moral realm as the law of gravity is in the physical world. This is why Paul cautions us: "*Do not be deceived. A man reaps what he sows. The one who sows to please his sinful nature will reap destruction; the one who sows to please the Spirit, from the Spirit will reap eternal life.*"[27]

What Are the Laws of the Harvest?

1. If we do not sow we will not reap. We are spared the destructive consequences of evil urges, fantasies, and ideas God's grace enables us to reject. However, this law also denies us of the harvest of blessing we would have reaped from the good we failed to do.

2   If we sow we will reap. Once the choice is made and the seed is planted the harvest is inevitable, whether it be evil or good.

3. If we sow we will reap what we sow. The kind of choices we make determines the nature of our harvest. God does not spare us the consequences of our choices.

4. If we sow we will reap more than we sow. This law should serve as a deterrent for doing evil, but an encouragement for doing good.

Mercifully, when our choices come from urges, fantasies, and ideas Satan suggests the harvest doesn't last forever. As Christine began to sow different kinds of choices she began to reap a different kind of harvest. Out of her pain she learned to distinguish more clearly the difference between options suggested to her mind by God and those coming from the enemy. This spiritual discipline resulted in wiser choices that gave her story a happy ending.

Unguarded Family Moments Can Be Disastrous.

Every family has its own unique sins. Through modeling we predispose our children to these sins. After all, modeling is the most powerful form of teaching. This is why certain vices seem to run in families. This danger is clearly presented in Scripture, *"Jeroboam. . . committed all the sins his father had done before him."*[28]

Early in life, then, the enemy begins to build his strongholds in us. Often the roots of these strongholds can be traced to tragic mistakes our parents have made or destructive behaviors they have modeled for us. For example, drug abuse, spousal abuse, and child abuse (physical, sexual, or emotional), all tend to run in families. This is the way Satan predisposes many of us to fall into the same sins that have scarred our parents' lives. These practices become closely guarded personal and family secrets. Satan builds his strongholds in these secrets of our lives and enforces them by our silence. When we break the silence we break the stronghold.[29]

The incredible speed of the mental process facilitates our fall. Verbal thought races ahead at three to four thousand words a minute...ten times faster than any human being can speak to us. Urges and fantasies rush through the mind at even more compelling speeds. If we are blind to the traps Satan has laid in our history, in a fraction of a second we can make an impulsive decision that can have devastating consequences for us and our family. . .sometimes for years to come.

There Is Hope for Us in Christ

In spite of the fact that we are fallen and sinful, God still loves us and longs to live in us. Regardless of the toll evil may have taken on our past, God offers us hope for a new future.

This is why He created a second Adam, who is the Lord from heaven. Charles Wesley celebrates that hope in his beloved Christmas carol, "Hark! The Herald Angels Sing." We would do well to make the closing words of that beautiful song our daily prayer:

". . . Adam's likeness now efface, Stamp Thine image in its place:

Second Adam from above, Reinstate us in Thy love."

This is what Christ came to do...reinstate us in God's love. He reconciled us to God by His death on the cross.[31] He rose from the dead; and in so doing removed every barrier between us and our heavenly Father. The Bible refers to Him as the "last Adam."[32] He is the obedient Adam . . . the sinless Adam . . . the triumphant Adam. He is all that the first Adam had the potential to be, and much, much more. He came to model for us the life God offers to us.

Being born into the family of the first Adam makes me a victim of sin, but it also opens up for me the possibility of being "born again" into the family of the last Adam who makes me a victor over sin. Just as we have borne the image of the first Adam, God can enable us to bear the image of the last Adam.[33] Through this miracle of grace, He not only makes it possible for you and me to house His Presence in our bodies, but also to express that Presence daily in our attitudes and actions.[34]

This means that you and I can change our presence. Isn't this encouraging? In the next chapter you will discover some practical steps you can take in bringing about this transformation.

FOOTNOTES

[1] Lews, C.S. A Mind Awake: An Anthology of C.S. Lewis; edited by Clyde S. Kilby. Harcourt, Brace, and World, Inc.: New York, NY, 1968, p. 105.
[2] John 10:10
[3] I Peter 5:8
[4] Ezekiel 28:15
[5] I Timothy 3:6; Isaiah 14:12-16; Ezekiel 28:12-19
[6] Ezekiel 28:15
[7] Revelation 12:4
[8] Isaiah 14:12-15
[9] Luke 10:18
[10] II Peter 2:4; Jude 6
[11] Matthew 25:41
[12] Matthew 16:18; I Peter 5:8
[13] Revelation 20:10
[14] II Corinthians 11:14
[15] Genesis 2:7, 20-25; 3:7
[16] Genesis 3:15
[17] Luke 10:18; Matt. 25:41
[18] I John 2:15-17
[19] Genesis 3:4
[20] II Corinthians 11:14
[21] Mark 13:22
[22] John 10:10
[23] Proverbs 14:12
[24] Romans 5:12
[25] Galatians 6:7-9
[26] I Corinthians 10:13
[27] Galatians 6:6-8
[28] I Kings 15:3
[29] James 5:16
[30] I Corinthians 15:47
[31] II Corinthians 5:18, 19
[32] I Corinthians 15:45
[33] I Corinthians 15:45-49
[34] Colossians 2:13-15

CHAPTER FIVE

YOU
CAN
CHANGE
YOUR
PRESENCE

Sometimes we let our friends talk us into doing things we would probably never do on our own. That's why I found myself standing gazing into a mirror unable to believe my own eyes. I looked twice as tall and twice as thin as I was. Two or three steps later when I looked again I was half as tall and twice as fat. Every few feet my appearance changed in some ridiculous way. The only comfort I found was that my friends looked just as ludicrous as I did.

I had been cajoled into a trip through a house of mirrors at a carnival. If you've ever had that experience, you know what a twisted view of yourself those mirrors can give you. The experience is hilarious, but there is a certain amount of relief that comes when you exit to a more familiar view of yourself and others.

Mirrors have ways of distorting life . . . some more than others. They can magnify or diminish. They can flatter or insult.

Such experiences make us aware that things and people are not always what they appear to be. You cannot always trust what you see. Perhaps that is why God made hearing, not seeing, the pathway to faith.[1]

Who Are the Mirrors in Your Life?

Each of us was born into his or her own personal house of mirrors. You did not arrive in this world with an album of self portraits already in your mind. The pictures you have of yourself were put together long after you were born. They came from the reflections you saw of yourself in the adult mirrors surrounding you; your parents and family, or those responsible for your care.

By the time you were five you had formed from those reflections a composite of yourself and others that you would carry into your adult life with very little editing.

As small children we do not become who we think we are. We become who we think other people, our parents or caregivers, think we are. Our presence grows out of this sort of "looking-glass" self formed from others' reflections of us.

The picture we create of ourselves from these reflections is a kind of self-portrait from which we view our world. Psychologists refer to it as our "self-concept." Your self-concept consists of the feelings and ideas you acquire about yourself from the words and actions of others, particularly members of your family.

No healthy parent would intentionally cripple their children with poor self-concepts. However, few adults understand the role they play in a child's formation of their self-concept.

It helps to remember that until children are about four years of age, they tend to believe everything an adult says to be absolutely true. This is why it is so important that adults be careful how they address little children. Even in jest, you should *never* tell a child that he or she is: dumb, stubborn, ugly, fat, stupid, lazy, mean etc. The mental pictures children form of themselves come from the words adults use to describe them. Is it any wonder that Jesus placed so much importance on the way adults speak and act toward children?[2]

A Healthy Self-Concept Is a Great Gift

One of the greatest contributions parents and older adults can make to the presence of children is to give them healthy ways of feeling and thinking about themselves. The impact these ideas and feelings have on a child is easily discerned by the time the child is old enough to enter kindergarten.

For example, one day, a little four-year-old girl accompanied her mother to her church office job. While the little girl was amusing herself with crayons and a coloring book an older transient man wandered in off the street and asked for financial assistance. He took a seat in the waiting room while the receptionist went to get the pastor.

The little girl innocently seeking to make a new friend said, "Hey, mister! What's your name?" The man just sat there in silence, staring at the floor. "I'm talking to you, mister," she said plaintively, but the man continued to ignore her.

Thinking he hadn't heard her, the child raised her voice and asked more loudly, "Hey mister! What's your name?" The man still never broke his silence.

Not to be denied, the little girl confidently proceeded to walk over to where the man was seated. She got down on her knees so she could look up into his face, tilted her head to make eye contact with him and asked again with a smile, "Hey, mister! What's your name?"

The man could no longer disregard her irresistible charm. His face broke into a gentle smile as he responded, "My name is George." The little girl replied, "My name is Denise, George. Nice to meet ya."

Then, satisfied that she had acquired a new friend, she got up, walked back to her crayons and coloring book and continued to chatter away with him from the other side of the room. The difference between her self-concept and his was obvious.

Children are not born with that kind of loving confidence. This little girl was projecting a presence that had its roots in four years of loving affirmation reflected to her through the feelings and words of the adult mirrors in her life.

Assurance, shame, love, guilt, joy, compassion, anger, compliance, defiance, shyness, inferiority, arrogance, humility, rebellion...all these traits and characteristics grow out of the interaction between small children and their parents. The observant kindergarten teacher can detect them within the first few days of school.

Other People Also Affect Us

Very early in life grandparents, day-care workers, siblings, playmates and other people interacting in our lives begin to have an impact on what we come to believe about ourselves. Few adults realize the powerful imprint they leave on children. I've already shared with you my abiding memories of Miss Kaller, my first grade teacher and the invaluable contribution she made to my self-concept. Unfortunately, not every adult in my childhood left such a positive imprint on me.

I also have vivid memories of Boyd's father. Boyd was my best friend from the third to the sixth grade. We were like Tom Sawyer and Huckleberry Finn. He spent a lot of time at my house and I spent a lot of time at his.

Boyd's mother always seemed kind and gentle to me. However, looking back at that family I strongly suspect Boyd's father abused her. When he was sober he would joke and tease with us, but when he was drunk he could be mean and explosive.

In one of his more jovial moments, Boyd's dad promised to take Boyd and me to a Saturday matinee movie. Those were the days when kids could see a western, a cartoon, and a chapter of a Lone Ranger serial for a dime. This was a big deal for us boys and we looked forward to it all week.

On Saturday afternoon, about an hour before we were to leave, I went over to Boyd's house. His dad had gone to town to have their car repaired, but he promised he would be back in plenty of time to take us to the show.

About every five minutes Boyd and I would look at the clock. Then, we would look out the window to see if his dad was in sight. A half hour or so before it was time to go our hopes began to sink. What if he forgot? The closer the time came for us to leave the more disheartened we became. After all, for eight-years-olds disappointments like this are major disasters.

The time we were to leave for the show came and went.

Boyd's dad still wasn't home. Two hours later, obviously drunk, he came staggering into the house slurring his greeting to us. He could see how let down we were, but he was too drunk to care and too drunk to be embarrassed. Boyd's mother was afraid to say too much because she didn't want to make him angry.

When I went home that night my little heart was heavy. I was not only disappointed because I didn't get to go to the show, but also, for the first time, I saw the pain and disappointment my friend had to live with every day. And more than a half-century later I can still recall the pain.

Boyd's father was an alcoholic. To this day, when I see a drunken man I get disgusted, frightened and angry, all at the same time. This is what a deep and lasting imprint Boyd's father made on my life during those years when I was in his home.

Whether you know it or not, your presence makes an imprint on others...for better or for worse. I'm sure Boyd's dad lived with far more pain than he inflicted on me. I don't know that he ever changed. I hope he did, but if he didn't it wasn't because he couldn't. It was because he wouldn't seek help for his problem...a problem that was devastating his life and his family...a problem that was treatable, but not self-correcting.

When people fail to change it's not because they *can't*. It's because they *won't*. And people who won't change are famous for telling sad stories about why they can't. Inevitably, these stories blame other people for their presence...a presence that is miserable for them to live with and a presence that makes those around them uncomfortable. You may not want to challenge their stories, but don't be taken in by them. Every day these same people are making the choice not to change.

Change Is Difficult and Uncomfortable

As long as a person can tolerate being the way they are they are not likely to change. They may admit they need to change. They may even say they want to change...but they continue choosing to remain the same until doing so hurts too much.

Look back over your own history. Times of major changes in our lives are usually marked by deep personal pain. Years ago, the Lord helped me discover that *until the pain of remaining the same hurts more than the pain of changing, people prefer to remain the same.*

Often, out of the crises of our lives comes not only the desire for change, but also the determination to change. During the same time when Boyd and I were best friends, I had a Sunday school teacher whom I dearly loved. Mr. Robertson was his name. Like Boyd's father, he had an unsavory history...a dirty mind, a filthy mouth and an insatiable thirst for alcohol. However, unlike Boyd's father Mr. Robertson was so desperate for change that he asked Jesus Christ to forgive him of his past and help him transform his life.

From that day on he never lost his determination to lead a changed life. Those who knew him when he was younger would never have recognized him as the same man who taught our boys' Sunday school class every week.

Mr. Robertson was the kind of Sunday school teacher who made ten-year-old boys wish every day were Sunday. Even though his military background gave him a commanding presence, he wasn't very tall. In fact, when he stood before the class none of us boys seemed short. His voice was somewhat raspy when he talked, but it was filled with love for us...and we felt it.

There were always ten or fifteen of us in the class. He knew each of us by name. And, the first few minutes of every class were spent telling Mr. Robertson about our week. He was one of the few adults in our lives who made us feel that what happened in the lives of ten-year-old boys each week was really important.

When he began to teach he had a way of telling Bible stories that kept us on the edge of our seats. Bible characters seemed to spring to life when Mr. Robertson talked about them. In my memory I still can see him slowly pacing back and forth in front of the class looking each of us in the eye as he talked.

When he closed the class in prayer he was careful to use words that we understood. And, he put those words together in ways that often brought us to tears.

I suppose one of the reasons all of us boys knew we were special to Mr. Robertson was that he had us out to his home every month for a baseball game. Those Saturday afternoons were filled with fun and always ended with soda pops, hamburgers, hot dogs, and ice cream.

If I were ever asked to teach a Bible class for ten-year-old boys I'd want to do it like Mr. Robertson did. This wholesome imprint on my life would be missing if he had not had a desire and determination to see his life changed by the Master.

I am glad Mr. Robertson decided to change. His presence made a big difference in my life. I'm sure he never knew what a lasting imprint he was leaving on me. But I look forward to letting him know some day in eternity what a difference he made on my life.

Creating the Need and Desire for Change

Since most of us give very little thought to the impact our presence has on others we may be unaware of any need to change. So how do we know if we should try to change our presence? How do you get in touch with your presence?

Begin by asking yourself questions like these:

- "What feelings are generated in me when I look at myself in the mirror?"
- "How do I feel about the person I'm with when I am alone?"
- "What feelings do I generate in others when they are around me?"

Reflecting on questions like these can produce some very

helpful insights and make you much more conscious of others' reactions to you.

Your Presence Flows Out of Your Self-Concept

You cannot change your presence without first changing your self-concept. When you change your self-concept you will change your presence.

Remember, you and I put together the mental pictures we have of ourselves out of reflections gleaned through the years we were growing up in our family's house of adult mirrors. Sometimes parents who have painful ways of looking at themselves are determined to give their children healthier self-concepts than they received from their parents. However, distorted self images tend to run in families. Pausing to reflect on the families your mother and father grew up in may help you better understand the way they saw themselves. Gaining some useful insights into the pain they may have lived with can help you view any personal pain they may have caused you more compassionately.

So from the images of us reflected by the significant adults in our childhood we put together the ways we have learned to feel and think about ourselves and the ways we believe others feel and think about us. When these reflections are flawed and distorted they have a seriously negative effect on our presence and cripple our ability to respond to the challenges of adult life in appropriate and productive ways.

Paul recognized this and reminded us that if we are going to celebrate a life filled with love we will have to put away these distorted childhood views of life.[3] The obvious inference here is that the laying aside of these crippling views is not something that automatically happens when we become Christians.

Many people enter the Kingdom of God with very twisted and distorted views of themselves and others. There is little joy and peace in their lives, even though they have received forgiveness for their sins. Consequently, their presence leaves much to be desired. After all, it is impossible to have a healthy presence and an unhealthy self-concept.

Taking Responsibility for Our Presence

Understanding the roles parents and other family members may have played in the formation of our presence is interesting and helpful, but it is not sufficient to change our presence. We will never change our presence by blaming our parents for it. *Our presence is a product of our choices over time.*

Not being happy with your presence is both good news and bad news. The bad news is that you are responsible for the choices that have produced it. The good news is that if you have the desire and the determination, you can change your presence by making better choices in the future.

Over time, through your daily choices, you can change both the nature and intensity of your presence. It will take time, but as you make healthier choices you will be rewarded with more satisfying consequences.

Introverts and Extroverts

Of course, to some extent the intensity of our presence will be affected by our genetic predisposition toward being either an introvert or an extrovert, but this really has little to do with having a healthy or unhealthy presence. These terms simply describe the way a person relates to people and life in general.

The extrovert tends to be more intense, initiates contact with people readily and gains meaning in life by actively interacting with his environment. On the other hand, the introvert tends to be less intense, internalizes his environment and finds meaning by interacting with it in his fantasy. Socially, the introvert is more likely to wait for other people to initiate contact.

Some people think that "introverts" are not as emotionally healthy as "extroverts" but this is not true. Having a healthy or unhealthy presence has little or nothing to do with whether one is an introvert or an extrovert.

Become Aware of the *Intensity* of Your Presence.

You take a major step in personal growth when you not only become aware of the nature of your presence, but also of the *intensity* of your presence. We talked about introverts and extroverts. When these personality traits are out of balance they become unhealthy. Introverts may become very passive and extroverts may become very assertive. Overly passive and overly assertive people can be very difficult to deal with.

Extremely passive people seem to enjoy keeping others guessing about what they are feeling and thinking. They may be too insecure to express openly how they feel even about insignificant things such as where they want to eat.

Trying to drive a car full of passive people to lunch can be very frustrating. The driver asks, "Where does everybody want to go for lunch?" And his passive passengers say, "We don't care. Just anywhere that's all right with you will be all right with us."

Taking them at their word, the driver responds, "I feel like Chinese food today." Immediately his passive passengers begin sending subtle, but specific signals that they certainly are not up for Chinese. Passive people would prefer others find out what they want by exhausting the list of things they don't want.

On the other hand, overly assertive people can be overwhelming. Often they are so intense they bowl people over, and seem to be totally unaware of it. They remind me of an energetic St. Bernard puppy. They are not content to let you know they love you, they feel they need to jump up on you and lick you in the face. They tend to smother and dominate. They would be much more effective if they could control their intensity and become more like a beagle or a basset hound.

Be careful not to misunderstand what I am saying. When I speak of assertive and passive people I am not speaking of leaders and followers. There is nothing wrong with being a good follower or an effective leader. But passive people are usually not healthy followers, and overly assertive people are usually not healthy leaders. Whether we lean more toward being an introvert or extrovert, we need conscious control over the intensity of our presence so that it does not become a problem for others.

The keys to change are *desire* and *determination*. Being aware of the need to change is not enough. We must have a *desire* to change. And, if the *desire* is to result in change it must be accompanied by the *determination* to change. Both are necessary. Neither is sufficient without the other. When both are present the question becomes, "Where do we begin?"

Begin By Changing Mirrors

If adults mirrored negative views to you when you were a child, then you will need to dismiss those distorted reflections and change mirrors. The Christian has two flawless mirrors from which to correct distorted images of themselves, distorted images of God and distorted images of others: the written Word and the Living Word.[4] We will have more to say about these mirrors later when we talk about "Making Your Presence His Presence."

Your presence has its roots in your ideas about yourself, about God and about others. So, if you want to change it you will need to take an objective look at the development of these three important concepts through your personal history and then bring them to the written Word and Living Word for editing and correction. Remember, we have not always held the views we have today about ourselves, about God, and about others. We certainly were not born with them. We have learned them. They are the product of conclusions we have chosen to draw from adult family reflections over time. Therefore we need to resist the temptation to blame others for brainwashing us or imposing their views on us. Many people get hung up here.

Even if we feel we had very few options in the past, it is important to realize that these views are no longer being forced upon us by others. We choose to continue our belief in them. Accept that responsibility.

Of course we were subject to the training of our parents, as they were to their parents. However, when we become adults we are responsible for reviewing the ideas we have about ourselves, God, and others to determine what adjustments need to be made in order to make these ideas conform to Scripture.

It is comforting to know that anything we have learned can be unlearned and something different learned in its place. Old learning can be replaced by new learning ...at any age! We are never too old to change!

We do not need to be permanent prisoners of what we learned about ourselves as children. Paul's testimony verifies this. His ideas about God, himself, and others changed drastically in the years following his confrontation with Christ on the road to Damascus...and so can ours![5] As adults we can replace unhealthy childish ways of looking at life with less distorted and healthier views.[6]

We begin by familiarizing ourselves with the battle we are fighting and the field on which it is waged. This is a spiritual battle that is waged in the mind to determine whether God's presence or Satan's will be expressed in our bodies. It begins at birth, if not sooner.

Earlier we talked about the influence of spiritual presence on our mental activities, our attitudes, and behavior. The Christian experiences eternal life emanating from Jesus as *an invisible power* to *impact on the mind to stimulate the brain to think in terms of urges, fantasies, and ideas that enhance and develop one's divine* potential. From Satan comes sin *"as an invisible power to impact the mind to stimulate the brain to think in terms of urges, fantasies, and ideas that detract from and destroys one's divine potential."*

Out of this mix, along with our natural urges, fantasies, and ideas we derive the concept of ourselves, God, and others. Here's a closer look at the four-step process through which these concepts are formed. A careful look at this process will help us understand how these concepts become distorted and what needs to be done to correct them:

1. Sensations. Sensations are the simple building blocks from which these ideas are formed: sights, sounds, feelings, tastes, and smells. The human brain is created to receive and react to these stimuli. However, none of us experience these sensations in a neutral or unbiased way. Each person perceives them different-ly. That is, each of us mentally processes these sensations in dif-ferent and unique ways. We may all see, hear, feel, taste, and smell the same things, but give them different meanings.

The difference in the meaning we ascribe to sensations is determined by our personal history which is where much of the distortion and bias has its roots.

2. Personal History. How does personal history affect the meaning we ascribe to sensations? For example, if we were in a room where there was the smell of smoke, people who have been in a life-threatening fire will interpret that smell differently than those who have not had such an experience.

People who have never been in a life-threatening fire are just likely to be curious about the smell. Whiffing the smoke a couple of times they are likely to ask, "Smell that? It smells like something is getting hot. Wonder what it could be?"

However, the person who has been in a life-threatening fire becomes aware that their pulse is racing and panicky feelings are beginning to flood their mind. They are saying, "I gotta get outa here! I gotta get outa here!" The smell is the same, but the meanings are different.

Birth order and the number of siblings is also an important part of our personal history. Birth order can make a difference in the way we develop a self concept. Oldest children are usually raised more strictly. They have a more severe conscience and often are more responsible than younger children. After all, they are the family's first free baby sitters.

Youngest children tend to be indulged more. They are accustomed to having others give in to their demands. They are more likely to expect others to care for them than they are to care for others.

Middle children have neither the senior status of the oldest child nor the favored status of the baby. Therefore, survival requires them to learn how to compromise and negotiate, and if they successfully master these skills, they may become more successful in their careers than either the oldest or youngest child.

Male children experience a different family history than female children. A boy who is raised with sisters is likely to be more feminine than if he had been raised with brothers. Likewise, a girl who is raised with brothers is likely to be more masculine than if she had been raised with sisters.

What was happening in your parent's marriage when you were growing up? Did either of them have an affair? Was there a divorce? Did you lose a parent or a grandparent in childhood? Did you lose close friends? Did your family move frequently? Did you suffer serious accidents while you were growing up? Were there debilitating illnesses or surgeries? Have you suffered painful rejections? Were you adopted? These are the kinds of things that can seriously affect your interpretations of life.

3. Interpretations. Remember, we do not live with the facts of our lives. We live with our *interpretation* of the facts of our lives. There's a limitless number of interpretations for every major event of our lives. Each event could be measured on a continuum of being very destructive to very creative:

Very Destructive   Very Creative

//

Satan wants you to choose your interpretations from the more destructive options he is presenting to you. And he will argue that his interpretations are the only ones consistent with the facts. However, God has a variety of very creative interpretations based on these same facts from which He wants you to choose.

Satan's destructive interpretations will stimulate urges, fantasies, and ideas in us that steal our peace and joy in life. God's creative options stimulate urges, fantasies, and ideas that keep us from bitterness and launch us into a more abundant life.[7]

Traumas Influence the Interpretation of Your Life

In reviewing your personal history, focus on the traumas of your life and the story you have chosen to tell yourself about them. Have the interpretations you have chosen brought you through the pain a better person, or have they left you bitter?

Earlier I shared with you that my birth was the cause of my mother's death. I cost my father his wife. My aunt lost a sister. And, my grandparents lost their baby girl . . . all because I was born.

It took several years for my family to absorb this loss. Their pain was too great for them to shield me from the facts. I knew what had happened to my mother before I was old enough to understand it. I cannot remember a time in my personal history when I was not aware that my birth killed my mother.

Until I invited Jesus Christ into my life I held myself personally responsible for her death. I believed that I was guilty of murdering my mother.

This haunted me in my secondary school years and left me feeling that I was an evil person. After all, I had killed my mother. At times, my anger about what happened and rebellion over it became the source of uncomfortable levels of depression.

Then shortly after I opened my life to Christ, He gave me a compelling *urge* to visit my mother's grave. During my childhood my aunt had often taken me there on Memorial Day to put flowers on my mother's grave. Nevertheless, the first time I went there by myself it was difficult for me to find it. However, the regular trips I began to make soon familiarized me with that part of the cemetery.

Sometimes I would just stand in front of the grave and focus on my mother's marker: "Ruby Katherine Dobbins, born 1908, died 1927". . . (just thirteen days following my birth). At other times, I would drive up beside her grave and sit in the car reflecting on the fact that she had died giving me birth. For most of us, our birthday is a day of celebration. But for me, it was often a cause for grief.

One day when I was nineteen I was standing at her grave, focusing on the fact that she was just my age when she died, and thinking that this was too young for anybody to die. That's when the Lord stimulated these thoughts in my mind: *"Not only did Jesus die for me, but my mother died for me too. How valuable my life must be. I must be sure to make it count for something."*

From that day to this I have never thought of myself as the murderer of my mother. Instead, I have seen my mother's death as adding to the value of my life. Had the enemy kept me hung up on his interpretation of my personal tragedy he would have destroyed me with bitterness.

The facts of my history have not changed. I know my birth cost my mother her life. But the Lord has helped me make that fact add to the value of my life and motivate me to try to make a difference in my world. He brought me through my pain a *better* man instead of a *bitter* man. Notice, one letter makes the difference between being *bitter* or *better*...and that one letter is "*i*." The choice is always up to us.

Life is experienced through sensations. These sensations prompt interpretations. And, interpretations provoke feelings.

4. Feelings. The feelings that dominate our spirit are not there by accident. They are the direct results of how we have chosen to interpret the events of our past.

Very early in life we gradually develop a spiritual inclination toward pessimism or optimism. The pessimist sees the angry side of God, the evil side of people, and the dark side of life. Satan is the purveyor of pessimism. The optimist sees the loving side of God, the good side of people and the bright side of life.

Pessimism predisposes us to choose our interpretations of life events from the *destructive* side. Optimism inclines us more toward creative interpretations the Lord stimulates in us.

The habitual ways we choose to interpret life leave an emotional residual in us. Over the years, life has an accumulative affect upon us. The longer we live the more full we become of the feelings that have grown out of the ways we have chosen to interpret life.

Jesus refers to this residual as a *treasure*. He says that this treasure can be good or evil. And, he tells us that the nature of our treasure will be revealed in our conversation. That is, out of the abundance of those feelings we have stored up in us we draw the topics and tone of our conversation.[8]

Anyone who listens carefully to our conversation can determine what fills our hearts. Our emotions become the mounting residual of our past interpretations of life.

However, regardless of how we have come to feel and think about ourselves in the course of growing up, as adults we can change.[9] Thank God. If the desire and determination are there, God will help us change our presence.

We cannot change the facts of our history. And that's all right, because our feelings about our past do not come from the facts. They come from the ways we have chosen to interpret the facts. When God helps us look at those facts differently and gives us a more creative way of interpreting them we will be more at peace with our past. How do we change the way we interpret trauma from our past?

Praying Through

Over the past thirty-five years I have seen hundreds of people change the way they feel and think about their past. In helping them change I have led almost all of them through this four-step process of "Praying Through."

1. Talk to God honestly about what is hurting you. This is not as simple as it sounds. Our church experiences often leave us feeling it is better to pretend things are going well than it is to be honest about what may be hurting us. We are not taught to talk to God honestly about our feelings.

As children and young people, we often feel we have to hide our feelings from our parents. So, as adults it is easy to assume that there is even greater need to hide our feelings from God. We may fear His punishment or it may be that we don't want to disappoint Him.

When I was instructing one lady how to pray through and urging her to pour out her anger and bitterness to God, she impulsively insisted, "But I don't want God to know I feel that way." So, I replied, "Yes, I'm sure it will come as a great shock to Him." Then we both had a good laugh.

The sooner we learn we can trust him with our honest feelings the sooner we can rid ourselves of the painful burden many of us carry. The Psalms where David is praying out his anger toward his enemies provide a good model for us in how to talk to God honestly about our feelings. In reading Psalms fifty-five to fifty-nine you will discover why God called David a man after His own heart.[10] He doesn't try to hide his intense anger toward his enemies. He prays God's vengeance on them.

Putting your honest feelings in writing is another helpful way to ferret out any root of bitterness that may be robbing you of peace and stealing your joy. Some people do this by journaling their feelings. Others write a letter they never intend to mail to the person or persons they see as the source of their pain. Sometimes they simply write the letter to God.

2. Pour your feelings out to God. Unless we deal with the painful events of our life as we experience them, in time the factual and emotional elements detach from each other. The emotional residual continues to poison our perception of life while we "forget" much, if not most, of the details. This is why writing is so helpful in "Praying Through."

The written description of what happened and the bitter memories involved allow the intellectual and emotional elements of the experience to be reunited. As you read what you have written to God it helps you get in touch with feelings provoked by these historic events, feelings that you may have suppressed for years. These feelings will infect your heart if they are not emptied from your spirit. You may not feel safe in expressing them to anyone but God, but you can express them to Him much like David did when he poured his soul out to God.[11]

Because "Praying Through" can be an intensely emotional experience you may want to reserve it for times when you are alone, especially if there are small children in your home. It could be confusing or even frightening for them to see you this involved in prayer.

3. Wait for God to comfort you by giving you a new and creative way to view your pain. Once you have cried your heart out and you are emotionally spent in God's presence, continue to wait reflectively before Him. In such moments of meditation God will open your spirit to a new way of looking at your old hurt.

I've shared with you how the Lord comforted me that day at my mother's grave. Just as He had a creative way for me to see this part of my history and freed me from the pain of knowing my birth was the cause of my mother's death, He has a creative way for you to see your history that will help you live more comfortably with the hurts from your past.

I cannot overemphasize the importance of following the emotional catharsis of "Praying Through" with a time of reflection and meditation. It is not enough to be relieved from the pain. We need a new way of looking at this part of our history that only the Lord can give us. This can only come to us as we open our inner ear to Him in meditation.

4. Spend time praising God for the new way He has given you to view your hurtful past. This puts God's comfort deep in your spirit and reinforces the new and creative way He helps you see your old hurts.

"Praying Through" should be seen as a process, not just an isolated experience. In some ways it is like peeling an onion. You deal with the pain layer at a time and you cry a lot.

Often, when you have prayed through one letter or journal entry you have written to God you will remember other dimensions of the experience. Write them down and pray them through. Date each entry and save them.

You know you have prayed through these parts of your history when there is no more to write. Once you have reached this place, ask God to give you a creative way to destroy what you have written.

You may want to put it in a metal container, set it on fire, and offer it up as a burnt offering to the Lord. You may want to tear it up in little pieces and flush them down the commode like you would the other wastes of your life. You may want to tear it up, put the pieces along with some rocks in a jar and throw it into some deep body of water.

The means you use is not important. The important thing is to create some symbolic reminder of God's faithfulness in freeing you from the pain and bitterness represented in what you wrote.

Getting the bitterness and pain out of our lives has a remarkable effect on our presence. You will notice it immediately...and so will your family. Within a few weeks everyone who knows you will feel the difference.

I have found it helpful to store up in my heart memories of God's love and compassion. They are new every morning![12] We are wiser to deal with the hurtful experiences of life as we encounter them. This helps us to guard our mind and spirit from residuals that would poison our presence.[13]

In the thirty-five years I have worked with people I have noticed some common hang-ups people develop that make their presence difficult for others. In the next chapter we will take a look at these hang-ups and explore some ways of breaking through them.

FOOTNOTES

[1] Romans 10:17
[2] Matthew 18:5-6
[3] I Corinthians 13:12
[4] James 1:23; II Corinthians 3:18
[5] Acts 0:1-23
[6] I Corinthians 13:11
[7] John 10:10
[8] Matthew 12:34, 35
[9] I Corinthians 13:11
[10] Acts 13:22
[11] Psalms 142
[12] Lamentation 3:22-23
[13] Proberbs 4:23

CHAPTER six

BARRIERS

TO

A

HEALTHY

PRESENCE

Evelyn, a petite attractively dressed thirty-two year old woman, entered my office rather apologetically and took the seat furthest from me. For several seconds she sat silently staring at the floor obviously depressed, waiting for me to begin our conversation.

As I talked with her I learned that for several months she had been having difficulty sleeping. Her medical doctor had prescribed an anti-depressant for her that was helping some, but Evelyn was still deeply depressed. When I asked what was troubling her, she said she didn't know, so I assumed she wasn't ready to tell me.

The first session revealed that this young mother of three had every reason for celebrating life. Her oldest child was thirteen, a daughter who had never given her any problems. She also had a ten-year-old girl she loved dearly and a boy who was delightfully eight. Her husband, Dawson, had a secure job in upper management with a local industry, so they had no financial problems. He adored her, was crazy about their children and was the kind of man who put his family first in his life.

They had grown up together in a small Midwestern town. They had been schoolmates since they entered kindergarten. Their families went to the same church where their fathers served as deacons.

Dawson and Evelyn were high school sweethearts who ran away and got married when they were eighteen. Doing the arithmetic to discover how long they were married when their thirteen-year old was born, I observed they hadn't had enough time to learn how to be married before they had to learn how to be parents. However, I kept this information to myself at the time.

As I began to inquire about her sexual history I noticed Evelyn becoming extremely uncomfortable. This is always a sensitive part of an intake interview, even for men. However, it was so obviously painful for Evelyn that I eased away from the subject and suggested we could cover this area in her next session. Then Evelyn said, "I know if I am going to get better there is something I have to share with you, but I just can't do it today."

At the time, I didn't realize how significant that statement would be. For the next two months at the end of each session I would hear something similar from Evelyn. Experience had taught me the wisdom of leaving the timing for such a self-disclosure up to the person.

On the day Evelyn decided to share her secret with me, I could tell by the way she entered my office. I knew she was going to open up a part of her life she had never let me hear. She began, "I know I'm not going to get rid of my depression until I get this off my chest. So, before I left home I made up my mind to tell you today."

This was Evelyn's story. She and her husband grew up in a very legalistic fundamental Christian church. Only church-sponsored social activities and entertainment were approved. Young people were discouraged from participating in gym classes, high school athletics or other school-sponsored social activities.

Since their fathers were deacons Dawson and Evelyn had access to keys of the church. This came in handy when musical groups or Bible quiz teams needed someone to unlock the church for them.

However, Dawson and Evelyn also turned this to their personal advantage. At times, they would sneak a key from one of their parents and use the church as a private place to carry on their love affair. During one of these times, Evelyn got pregnant.

Fran was Evelyn's closest girlfriend. Fran knew everything that was going on in Evelyn's life. She knew about the meetings she and Dawson were having in the basement of the church, and she knew when Evelyn got pregnant. In fact, Fran helped Evelyn and Dawson elope.

Of course, it wasn't long before the secret was obvious to everyone in the church. Even though Dawson and Evelyn were married the pastor decided something had to be done because they weren't married when the pregnancy occurred. So, he forced the two of them to publicly confess their wrongdoing in front of the congregation on a Sunday morning. I can only imagine how humiliating this must have been. He also required their fathers to resign as deacons of the church. Having suffered this kind of treatment, I could not believe that both families continued going to that church, but they did.

After their baby was born, Dawson and Evelyn began to worry about how they were going to explain their wedding date to their daughter when she became a teenager. They knew that if the records remained as they were she would discover that they had not been married long enough to make her birth legitimate. So they arranged to have their marriage certificate edited to make it appear they had been married a year before their daughter was born so they could shield her from this embarrassment. Of course, Fran helped Evelyn get this done.

Several years later, Fran and her husband were transferred to another part of the country. Evelyn stayed in contact with Fran for a long time, but they both led busy lives and finally lost touch with each other. However, Evelyn recently had learned that Fran and her husband were being transferred back into the area. Instead of this being great news, Evelyn became horrified with the thought that Fran might feel obligated to be honest with their thirteen-year old daughter about the truth she and Dawson had tried so hard to protect her from.

Evelyn took the whole session to tell me this story. Several times she broke into tears. When she finished I let her have a few seconds to regain her composure. Then I said to her,

"Is that all?" With a look of disbelief she said, "What do you mean, is that all? Isn't that enough?"

It was obvious that Evelyn still felt a sick need to be punished. She had never dealt adequately with the guilt surrounding her premarital involvement with Dawson. So I said, "Evelyn, at the time did you ask the Lord to forgive you for having sex with Dawson?" "Yes," she replied. "Do you believe that He did?" "Yes," she insisted, "but how can I ever forgive myself?"

Hearing this tortured woman say that gripped me with such anger at the Accuser, I said, "Oh, are you telling me that your conscience is more difficult to satisfy than the holy nature of God?"

Startled, she protested, "I don't know what you mean."

"I mean," I continued, "the blood of Jesus was punishment enough to satisfy a holy God that He could be just in forgiving you, but now you tell me your conscience is demanding something more. Is your conscience more holy than God's nature? Must God send another Son to die just so your conscience can feel that your sins have been sufficiently punished?"

At this point, Evelyn sobbed through her tears, "I have never seen it that way. Of course, Calvary should be enough for my conscience."

I wish I could describe that liberating moment for you. Evelyn's countenance changed. Her depression obviously lifted. A look of peace and joy was reflected in her gentle smile. We took a few minutes to celebrate the moment and thank God for the healing it brought to Evelyn.

I urged Evelyn to call Fran and tell her the agony she put herself through once she knew Fran and her husband were moving back into the area. By the next time I saw her, she and Fran were talking regularly and looking forward to resuming their friendship.

A month later I saw Evelyn for the last time. She was sleeping well. Her energy had returned. Her doctor had taken her off the anti-depressant. She had finally broken through the barriers of suspicion and guilt to celebrate a healthy presence for the first time in her married life.

However, among very sincere and devout Christians there are many who never do develop the kind of wholesome, healthy presence Christ died to provide for us. Not every one deals with the same barrier that proved so difficult for Evelyn.

Over the years, I have observed eight common barriers that seem to hang people up and hinder their spiritual growth and development. If any of these are recognizable in your own life, I hope you will find the practical suggestions for overcoming them helpful in breaking through these barriers to the celebration of a healthy presence with your family and friends.

1. Suspicion. Friendship and intimacy are among life's most rewarding experiences. However, trust is an essential element in building this kind of pleasurable relationship. Unfortunately, the suspicious person is unable to trust.

There are times when suspicion is normal and healthy. For example, if a person lives in a neighborhood where the crime rate is high, being wary is essential to survival. However, most people living in these areas can still develop the level of trust necessary to enjoy healthy relationships with their family and friends.

If your spouse gives some evidence of having an affair, then suspicion is healthy until guilt or innocence can be established. Whatever steps are necessary to determine this should be taken as quickly as possible. In either event someone is going to be hurt. After all, there are few things more painful than discovering your spouse is having an affair; or, being suspected of having an affair when you aren't.

However, there are people so fearful of intimacy and emotional abandonment they rely on suspicion to keep themselves safe. In the background of these people there is usually a history of repeated rejection and betrayal or an obvious lack of nurturance during the pre-verbal years of life. In either event, the suspicious person is torn between the pain of loneliness and the fear of being vulnerable. Breaking through this barrier can be very difficult.

However, many people can be helped to break through this barrier by understanding the stages involved in building a relationship. Just being able to apply the following structure can help a person feel more in control of the process and quiets their apprehension.

Most friendships grow through four stages. During the initial stage you are simply sampling the interpersonal chemistry, trying to discover if you resonate with each other's vibes. Usually, you have to be with a person two or three times before you can come to some conclusion about this.

During the second stage you risk trusting the person with some innocuous information about yourself and see if they are willing to do the same. In building a friendship, it is wise to trust a person with only the same degree of intimate information about yourself, as they are willing to share with you about themselves.

Once the bridge of trust begins to build, both of you will have a greater need to be with each other. Then you will begin to see each other more frequently, which brings you into stage three. During this time you will talk more often on the telephone and do more things together.

In stage four of the friendship, you will begin to do things for the other person and they will begin to do things for you. This will create greater comfort in the relationship. You will feel safer in revealing more personal things about yourselves to each other...and the circular procedure will continue

Notice, the reciprocation in this process! If the other person does not respond with information about themselves when you confide information about yourself, see that as a warning sign and don't over-invest in the relationship. If the other person does not do things for you when you do things for them, this is a strong indication he or she is a "taker" not a "giver." If this is a relation-ship potentially leading to marriage, back out before you get hurt. Don't over-invest in a relationship that is not reciprocal.

People who have had little or no nurturance during the pre-verbal years of life face a different and more difficult chal-lenge. They not only lack the ability to trust, they have never developed the ability to be bonded to another human being.

The brutality of the first century leaves me feeling that many early Christians came from such backgrounds. Then, how did these early Christians become so famous for their love?[1] God supernaturally imparted His love to them.

Perhaps the most powerful element in healthy conver-sions is a revelation of God's love for us. Paul says, "God has poured out His love into our hearts by the Holy Spirit."[2] This kind of love drives out the fear of being hurt by people and builds one's ability to trust.[3] How can a person be open to such love?

In your devotions, study the word "love" in the New Testament. Begin with I John 4. Keep a journal of your findings and review them prayerfully. Take advantage of those moments in worship when you feel most vulnerable to God by earnestly asking the Holy Spirit to flood the center of your being with God's love. An infusion of God's love for you can help you break free from the barrier of suspicion.

2. Dependency. Most of us have had more than our share of experiences with adult "leaners." These people are so filled with self-doubt they have never been able to stand on their own two feet. They have enormous needs for reassurance and sup-port. Even the most compassionate of their friends grow weary in trying to satisfy these needs.

At first, having a person seek our instruction or solicit our opinions feeds our need to be needed. However, sooner or later, we find their demands on us overwhelming, draining and somewhat of a nuisance.

Overly dependent people are like adult children who

need someone to hold their hand when they cross the street. They often are full of shame and self-doubt. Most likely, they have been raised by parents who would rather do things for their children than to teach their children how to do things for themselves.

These children grow up expecting other people to think for them and do things for them just like their parents did. And, as long as you are willing to do things for them they will be willing to let you.

You are helping them help themselves and build some healthy self-confidence when you encourage them to find their sufficiency in Christ. By insisting that these people do things for themselves and complimenting them for doing things well you can wean them away from their dependency and help them become more self-sufficient. Even though we all are aware that without Him we can do nothing, these Christians need to discover that with His help they can do all things.[4]

3. Self-Consciousness. Usually, these are bright and talented people, but they have zero confidence in their intelligence, judgment, or ability. Exercising any initiative in life leaves them flooded with guilt and an overwhelming fear of failure. They are paralyzed by self-consciousness.

What is self-consciousness? It is the feeling of being observed but not approved. It has its roots in the fourth and fifth year of life when children so desperately want their parents to brag on what they do. Self-consciousness is usually engendered by perfectionistic parents who leave children feeling they are seldom if ever able to live up to the parents' expectations.

Our Heavenly Father is not difficult to please. People raised by perfectionistic parents find this hard to believe, but Jesus assured us that His yoke is easy and His burden is light.[5] Paul reassured Timothy that God has not given us a spirit of fear, but of power, love, and a sound mind. As they are used here the words "sound mind" have nothing to do with mental health. They refer to the ability to think clearly and express oneself clearly.[6] Self-consciousness clouds the mind and paralyzes the voice. Paul wanted Timothy to be free from this barrier.

If you battle self-consciousness, instead of imagining your perfectionist parents looking and listening disapprovingly at what you are doing and saying, begin to picture the Lord looking at your best efforts with a smile on His face. He wants to help you break free from the barrier of self-consciousness into the liberty of a self-confidence rooted in Him.

4. Inferiority. Once we start school, feelings of inferiority become a threat to us. Our scores and grades begin to be compared with our siblings and peers. American children are overburdened with the urge to compete. Often this flame is fanned by family and friends. The challenge is to accomplish the most and be the best. From there it is so easy to begin relating our self-worth to our achievements.

When others do more or better than we do having good feelings toward them is difficult. Their high level of performance often results in us discounting the value of our accomplishments. This can cripple us with painful feelings of inferiority.

This is why Paul tells us that it is never wise to determine the value of what we do by comparing it with what others are doing.[7] If you tend to get caught up in this game of competitive comparisons mentally withdraw from it. Refuse to base your self worth on what you do or what you have.

The worth of every child of God was established at Calvary. None of us are worthy of that price, but that is what God was willing to pay for our redemption. God can't love you any more than Calvary and He won't love you any less. Keep your heart fixed on the price God paid to make you His child and remind yourself that He doesn't have any inferior children.

Don't covet others' gifts. Discover the gifts God has given you and develop them. You will find them in your head, your hands, or your heart.

If you can deal with high level abstractions and complex

concepts, obviously you have intellectual gifts. If your visual-motor skills are exceptional, then you have gifted hands. If you are thrilled by music, art, and poetry these indicate your gifts are in your heart. Each set of these gifts can be translated into exciting and fulfilling careers or vocations.

Identify your gifts. Develop them to levels of excellence. Then, do your best to use them humbly in serving God and others.

5. Gender Confidence. All of us have been around people who are uncomfortable with their gender role. Feeling good about being male or female is closely related to your feelings about your body. These feelings are largely formed during early childhood and adolescence. These are the two times in life when we are more likely to compare our bodies with others of the same sex.

When small children bathe with their parents they become almost hypnotically fixated on the parent's mature genitals. One little three-year old girl bathing with her mother broke free from her spell by saying, "Mommy, how's come you're so fancy and I'm so plain?" The wise mother smiled and reassured her little girl by telling her, "When you grow up and become a woman you will be fancy just like Mommy."

When little boys are dressing or undressing with their Dad and compare their genitals with their father's they seem so tiny. The thoughtful father shares with his son that when he was a little boy he was tiny, too. And, promises the child that when he grows up his genitals will be big like his dad's. Remarks like this help build the child's confidence in his sexual identity.

One of the cruelties of life is the disparate schedule adolescent growth imposes upon us. Peers often envy those who are blessed with premature development. The early appearance of secondary sex characteristics usually gives teens confidence in their gender identity. However, this older appearance often results in adults holding them more accountable than is fair for someone their age.

On the other hand, those who have to deal with a delayed

adolescence are embarrassed by their lack of secondary sex characteristics. This becomes especially sensitive for them when they compare their bodies with their peers' during gym classes or sleepovers. Sometimes the mental image from scenes like this become fixated in a person's memory and irrationally haunts them throughout life leaving them feeling less manly or womanly than their peers. I've seen great relief come to men and women in therapy by simply reminding them that if the same group were in gym class together at this point in their lives those embarrassing differences would have disappeared.

In a cartoon I once saw, a scrawny little guy was standing in front of a mirror flexing his muscles. There was a big smile on his face. The caption read, "I may not be much, Baby, but I'm all I've got." You can't beat that for a wholesome body attitude.

We will be happier if we just accept the body our genes have created, learn the roles our society ascribes to people of that gender, and celebrate our masculinity or femininity. Don't get hung up comparing yourself with others. You're the only one God has like you. Remember, our body is God's gift to us and the life we live in it is our gift to Him. It's the beauty of the life that counts.

6. Selfishness. Generally, people can be divided into two groups: givers and takers. These characteristics are discernible by the careful observer before a person graduates from high school. Givers and takers deserve each other, but they seldom find each other.

The giver's need to give attracts them to people who need to take. Of course, the giver also likes to receive. They assume that if they give enough to the taker, sooner or later, the taker will give back to them. But a giver can never give enough to make a giver out of a taker. Only God can make a giver out of a taker, and when this happens it is a miracle.

Jesus taught that it is more blessed to give than it is to receive. Generosity is an inevitable trait of a healthy Christian.

One way to break through the barrier of selfishness is to have a goal of giving something to someone every day from which no return is expected. It may be the change the person needs who is in front of you at the convenience store. It may be a thoughtful reminder of friendship. Or, it may be just a smile.

The rewards of giving will encourage you to develop this grace in your life. One Christmas season, my wife Priscilla and I pulled into a gas station to fill our car's gas tank. Priscilla struck up a conversation with a woman who was using the adjoining pump.

In the course of the conversation the woman told Priscilla that her work had not been steady so she had decided to forego having a Christmas tree. She could use the money she saved from the tree to make Christmas a little nicer for her children.

Priscilla put a twenty dollar bill in the woman's hand and told her we wanted her children to have a tree this Christmas. At first, she didn't want to take it, but Priscilla insisted. This was one of the best twenty-dollar investments we ever made in our own happiness. Giving brings its own reward!

7. Stagnation. There's a world of difference between a sparkling brook and a stagnant pond. Sometimes as we approach midlife we lose the sparkle in life. We allow ourselves to settle into routines that are boring and disgustingly stagnant.

This was Charles' complaint. He had an excellent job in middle management with a major automaker, but his upward mobility was limited and his job was no longer challenging for him. He lamented, "I don't want to spend the rest of my life like this." I asked Charles, "What would you like to do with the rest of your life?"

I'm not sure I was prepared for the answer. "I have always wanted to be a mortician," he replied. "Well," I said, "Why not save the money you will need, apply for acceptance into mortuary school, and go for it."

Today, Charles owns the leading funeral home in a small

midwestern town. All he needed to cure the stagnation in his life was a little encouragement.

What are your unfulfilled dreams? Why not make them come true? Going back to school or training for a new vocation can rejuvenate your life and add some much needed sparkle to your presence.

You're never too old to dream. Remember, Grandma Moses never knew she could paint until she was in her seventies. Colonel Sanders hadn't made his first million until he was old enough to draw Social Security.

8. Despair. The last two decades of life reveal how well we have lived. They can be our brightest and best or our darkest and worst. The difference will depend largely on how we have chosen to remember our years.

When Paul looked back on his life he was satisfied with how he had lived it. He didn't require himself to have fought a perfect fight. He was content with a good one. He was comforted by the conviction that he had completed his course with his faith intact.[8] Being comfortable with your past is vital to a healthy presence in your later years.

Nothing is as pathetic as an older person full of regrets. They tend to be cynical, critical, and generally unpleasant to be around. They can't celebrate the years they have left because they can't let go of the past.

Paul had things in his past that could have overwhelmed him with regret if he had chosen to dwell on them. He was a persecutor of Christians.[9] He made widows out of Christian wives and orphans of their children. Had he chosen to recall these events in his later years he would have drowned himself in tears of remorse and regret.

Reviewing the past is normal for an older person, but it is devastating to see them get hung up on the things that went wrong. There are those things in everyone's past, but we don't have to focus on them. Paul chose to forget the events of his history that could have shrouded his remaining years in disappointment and regret. He kept his eye on the future, determined to seize the prize he knew awaited him.[10]

Nothing is as inspiring as the presence of an older person who can trace God's hand of mercy and grace through their history and is at peace with their past. Their wisdom is an inspiration to the young and their joy is a monument to life.

Breaking Through Emotional Barriers

Now that we have outlined several emotional barriers, here are two practical suggestions for overcoming and breaking through these barriers.

1. The New Birth. Breaking through the emotional barriers outlined in this chapter obviously requires a personal relationship with Jesus Christ. If you have never given your life to Christ then this is your first step toward the healing you need. Ask Jesus to forgive you of your sins. Believe that He does. Receive Him as your Savior. It's just that simple.

Being "born again" does not mean just "trying harder" or "turning over a new leaf." It means that the part of you that was insensitive to God is made alive so that He can speak to you through your urges, your fantasies, and your ideas. Just as your first birth sensitized you to the natural world of sights, sounds, feelings, tastes, and smells, being "born again" sensitizes you to the realities of the spiritual world. When you are born again you become a member of "a new creation in Christ Jesus." This is why he was crucified and raised from the dead.[11]

2. Attend a healthy biblically-based church. If you are going to continue to overcome the emotional barriers of your life, you will need to become a part of a healthy Bible-centered church where you can take the necessary steps toward putting the pain of your past behind you. This will bring a dramatic change in the way you see yourself and in the impact your presence has on other people.

Your choice of a church is critical to the kind of presence you develop. Choose a church whose pastor is an effective teacher of the Word of God, and a model for Christian living. Each of us needs to be taught by another.[12] However, you will find it difficult to be spiritually healthier than the person you choose as your pastor/teacher.

Most pastors are spiritually healthy and committed to helping their parishioners grow and develop a healthy presence. However, there are people in occupational ministry who are not emotionally and spiritually healthy. Whatever church you choose, it is important for you to be sure the pastor is healthy and has a healthy relationship with his or her spouse and children.

Sound biblical teaching helps you grow, but being in an unhealthy spiritual environment will stunt your spiritual growth, or worse, give you false ideas about God and His character. In a large church the best model may be a dedicated lay person, or a staff pastor who has the time to nurture you. But the senior pastor still needs to be someone who can provide you with solid biblical teaching every week.

Many believers also get involved in a small group. Here, they study God's Word, pray together, confide in one another, and hold each other accountable for spiritual growth.

How Do You Know if Your Faith Is Healthy?

There is no shortage of sick religion in our world. It is vitally important that you develop a healthy faith. In the emergence of a healthy faith you should be able to observe the following characteristics:

1. A healthy faith is affirmed in fellowship.[13] Christianity is defined in community. A healthy faith will never isolate you. "But if we are living in the light of God's presence, just as Christ does, we have fellowship and joy with each other..." I Jn. 1:7a (Living). Be sure you are involved with other believers who are committed to growing toward spiritual maturity.

2. A healthy faith defines God as love. Even God's justice is tempered by His love.[14] "But if a person is not loving and kind, it shows that he doesn't know God—for God is love." I Jn. 4:8 (Living) Churches that preach lots of condemnation and fear are unhealthy. If you are "dangled over hell on a rotten stick" every Sunday, you will have a warped image of Father God.

3. A healthy faith enhances self-worth.[15] We are unworthy of our Savior's death, but because of Calvary no human being is worthless. Healthy people know the difference between feeling "unworthy" and feeling "worthless." "For you know that it was not with perishable things such as silver or gold that you were redeemed....but with the precious blood of Christ.." I Peter 1:18-19 (NIV)

4. A healthy faith helps you face reality. An unhealthy faith allows you to escape reality.[16] Many "religious" people are running away from life. Some hide behind the mask of a superficial spirituality. But a healthy faith will cause you to honestly confront the reality of your life, and help you enact the changes you need to make. You can face reality, "because greater is he that is in you, than he that is in the world." I Jn. 4:4b (KJV)

5. A healthy faith prepares you for the future. Change is one of the predictable characteristics of the future.[17] A healthy faith gives you the flexibility to adapt to change.

6. A healthy faith enables you to deal with stress and anxiety.[18] The greater the stress the more divine grace and strength God pours into our lives.[19] "...In all these things, we are more than conquerors through him who loved us. For I am convinced that neither death nor life, neither angels or demons, neither the present nor the future, nor any powers, neither height nor depth, nor anything else in all creation, will be able to separate us from the love of God that is in Christ Jesus our Lord." Romans 8:37-39 (NIV)

7. A healthy faith finds joy in giving.[20] Gratitude for God's generous provision for us provides a stimulus for healthy giving. We do not give to receive. We share with others God's generous treatment of us. We give freely because we have so freely received. "It is more blessed to give than to receive." Acts 20:26b (KJV)

8. A healthy faith manages anger constructively.[21] The healthy believer is quick to confess when their misdeeds hurt and anger others and are just as quick to forgive when others' misdeeds hurt and anger them. "Don't let the sun go down with you still angry——get over it quickly." Eph. 4:26 (Living)

9. A healthy faith balances work and play.[22] Keeping God first, our spouse and children second, and our work third in our priorities should allow us time for rest and recreation. Deviation from these priorities over a long period of time will cost us dearly.

10. A healthy faith loves and forgives others. Nothing will contaminate your presence more than accumulating the festered sores of the past in your spirit. "And be kind to one another, tenderhearted, forgiving one another, even as God for Christ's sake has forgiven you." Eph. 4:32 (NKJV)

Once the barriers to growth and maturity are broken in your life, you are ready to pick up the challenge of making your presence His Presence. In the next chapter we will be examining the process by which this transformation takes place and defining our role in it.

FOOTNOTES

[1] John 13:35
[2] JRomans 5:5
[3] I John 4:18
[4] John 15:5; Philippians 4:13
[5] Matthew 11:30
[6] II Timothy 1:7
[7] II Corinthians 12:12
[8] II Timothy 4:7
[9] Acts 22:4; 26:11; I Timothy 1:13
[10] Philippians 3:13
[11] I Corinthians 15:1-4
[12] Acts 8:30-34
[13] I John 1:7-9
[14] I John 4:7-8
[15] Mark 8:36-37; I Peter 1:18-19
[16] I John 4:4
[17] I Corinthians 9:19-23
[18] Philippians 4-9
[19] II Corinthians 12:7-10
[20] Acts 20:35
[21] Ephesians 4:26
[22] Matthew 6:14-15; Ephesians 4:32

CHAPTER SEVEN

MAKING

YOUR

PRESENCE

HIS

PRESENCE

In 1889 a normal healthy baby boy was born to aspiring Austrian parents. Over time, this innocent little baby would become one of the twentieth century's greatest embodiments of evil. Before his death this maniacal genius unleashed a genocidal tirade that annihilated over six million Jews. When added to the other victims of his paranoid dreams for conquering the world he would take more human life than any person in modern history. Even though I haven't named him, you know I am talking about Adolph Hitler. His evil presence identifies him.

There was no way to predict this child was headed for such a dark and ominous future. His parents certainly could never have anticipated it. They were decent hard-working middle class Austrians. The boy didn't grow up with the ambition to be one of the world's most evil men.

How did it happen? How did Adolph Hitler become the greatest mass murderer of modern history? Gradually, through the choices he made, he yielded his life to the urges, fantasies, and ideas stimulated in him by Satan, the one who steals, kills, and destroys.[1] Satan found in Adolph Hitler a mind and body willing to express evil's destructive presence and the rest is history.

In 1918, on the eastern seaboard of the United States another healthy baby boy was born in Charlotte, North Carolina. Over time, this little boy would become the most famous Christian in the twentieth century. In the course of his ministry as Christianity's most successful evangelist he would lead millions of people to Jesus Christ...more than any other person in the history of the church. Even though I haven't mentioned his name you know I am talking about Billy Graham.

No one could have predicted that this child would become such a power for Jesus Christ, not even his godly parents. As a boy, Billy was too shy and modest to entertain this kind of ambition for himself.

How did it happen? How did Billy Graham become the most effective evangelist in the history of Christianity? Gradually, through his choices, he yielded his life to the creative urges, fantasies, and ideas stimulated in his mind by Jesus Christ who found in Billy Graham a mind and body willing to express His creative Presence on earth.

At an early age Billy opened his life to Jesus Christ. By the time he was twenty-one he was an ordained Baptist minister. Later, he left the pastorate to become an itinerant evangelist . . . and the rest is history.

This study in contrasts of character brings into sharp focus the role personal choice plays in determining the destructive or creative nature of one's presence. Billy Graham is an example of what God can do through the body of just one person who is willing to express the urges, fantasies, and ideas of His creative Presence. On the other hand, Adolph Hitler shows us the tragic destructive potential of just one person who chooses to give himself over to satanic urges, fantasies, and ideas.

Can you imagine how different the world might have been had Hitler chosen to glorify God in his body instead of choosing to abandon his divine potential for a demonic one? He turned his back on the future God had designed for him and opened his spirit to Satan. As a consequence, the human race not only suffered the destructive impact of his demonic potential, but also was denied the creative impact of his divine potential. This is the tragedy of not allowing our lives to opened up to God's creative Presence. It essentially means we are lost.

What Does It Mean to Be Lost?

Traditionally we associate being lost with a person going

to hell when they die. Although this is true, being lost is far more tragic than this. When someone dies without having developed a relationship with God the human family is denied the unique physical expression of God's presence that person was born to express.

Think of what this means! The dimension of Christ's presence that person was born to express is forever lost . . . to that person, to the human race, to angels, to God and to the universe. *People who are lost commit the ultimate sin of omission . . . they chose to deny God a means of expressing His presence through their body.*

Life's Highest Purpose

God created human beings to give physical expression to His presence on earth. This was His plan for doing His will on earth as it is in heaven.[2]

The human race was not created to populate heaven. Heaven was well populated long before Adam and Eve.[3] They were created to populate earth with beings uniquely designed for expressing God's presence on this planet to bring it back under divine dominion.[4]

Let's set our thinking straight. Our body was not created so our soul and spirit could go to heaven. Our soul and spirit go to heaven because, through God's mercy and grace, we have chosen to house God's presence in our body on earth.

God's genius in designing the human race for this purpose is seen in the uniqueness He gives each person. In the history of the human race no two people have ever been totally alike...not even "identical twins." As frightening as the prospects of cloning may be it can never produce people who are exactly alike.

You Are a Miracle!

You, my friend, are one of a kind...a mathematical miracle! When you look at yourself in the mirror, remember that the person looking back at you is a unique miracle of God. How unique? Astonishingly unique!

Before your mother was born there were 1,500,000 potential human beings in her little ovaries. No two of these ova were genetically alike. By the time she reached womanhood, her body had absorbed all but 40,000 of them. In the course of her fertile years, she would bring to fruition only about 300 to 350 of them. So, from your mother's side the chance that you would be born the person you are is one in 1,500,000.

When your mother and father made love, 150,000,000 to 300,000,000 of his sperm entered her body. No two of these shared the same genetic code. So the likelihood that you would be born who you are from your father's side is one in 150,000,000 to 300,000,000. In order to determine your statistical uniqueness you would have to multiply one in 1,500,000 by at least one in 150,000,000. These odds are staggering!

You are not only a statistical miracle. The process of your gestation and birth is just as incredible. Once you were conceived the miracle of your life continued to grow inside your mother. From a speck no bigger than the head of a pin with no recognizable physical features you grew into a baby human being ready for birth in just nine months.

During that time you developed an optical system that would let you see the beautiful colors of your world in three dimensions. You arrived with your own surround sound system capable of hearing in Dolby stereo. You came equipped with a little chemistry laboratory capable of first turning fluids and then solids into bone, muscle, flesh and hair. The gestation process that shaped and formed your body in your mother is a miracle!

Your Body Is Important to God

Why did God create such an awesome magnificent body? Because your body is important to Him! Your body is the means

He has chosen for expressing His presence on earth. Adam was not created a bodiless soul or spirit. He was given a body from the dust of the earth, and breath from God to physically express the Presence of God on earth. *God has decreed it to be impossible to accomplish His divine purpose on earth without human bodies!*

The uniqueness of your body makes it possible for you to develop an expression of Christ's Presence that has not been duplicated by any other child of God in the history of the Church. Jesus alone is capable of expressing all the fullness of Deity in bodily form, but He shares a unique portion of that fullness with every person who is "born again."[5]

What Do We Lose By Not Allowing God's Creative Presence in Us?

No one else will ever be capable of expressing the unique physical dimension of Christ's Presence you were born to reflect. By choosing not to allow that expression of Christ to grow and develop from your life the world will be denied the opportunity for ever knowing what it might have been. As you can see, when a person dies without discovering and developing this divine potential heaven and earth are the poorer for it.

This is the greatest tragedy of being lost. However, it seldom is mentioned. When we think about a person being lost we are so overwhelmed by the thought of that person suffering in hell forever, we fail to grieve over the loss of their potential Christ-likeness here and now. Satan has stolen this treasure from them, a treasure more valuable than the wealth of the whole world.[6] And Christ has been denied this person's reflection of His Presence in the ages to come. Although this in no way detracts from the glory of Christ's Presence, it does deprive Him of the person's eternal reflection of His presence.

Your Body Is for the Lord

Paul reminds us that the *body* is for the Lord.[7] He says it is the temple of the Holy Spirit.[8] What does this mean? The body is the place where the Holy Spirit resides.

The only way others can know He resides in us is for us to glorify God in our bodies.[9] This is why Paul pleads with us to present our bodies to God so we can be transformed by the renewing of our minds and Christ can express His life through us.[10] He wants our attitudes and behavior to physically express His presence so that others can recognize Him in us.

How Does This Transformation Take Place?

It begins with a supernatural act and continues through a supernatural process. I have spent much of my adult life searching for a clearer understanding of this process. What follows is an attempt to share with you what I have learned in hopes that it will prove to be of practical help in making your presence His presence.

We don't need special understanding or assistance to give physical expression to Satan. Until we are "born again" it is normal for us to express Satan's presence. Our fallen nature inclines our will toward his urges, fantasies and ideas.

However, before we can physically express the presence of Christ we must experience the miracle of a new birth—a spiritual birth.

Why Must We Be "Born Again?"

Christ came to begin a new race of human beings. The only way for us to participate in the life of this new creation is to be born into it.[11] You can see why this is necessary once you ask yourself, "How did we acquire our fallen nature from the first Adam?" The obvious answer is that we were born into his race. Every person who is born into the first Adam's race shares in his fallen nature.

So if we are going to share the un-fallen nature of the Second Adam (Jesus), we must be born into his race. After all, it is not until our natural birth provides us with a body designed to communicate with the natural world that natural things become real to us. How can spiritual things be real to us until our new birth provides us with a regenerated spirit capable of communicating with God?[12]

Just as a child must be born into the first Adam's race before he or she can begin to live the fallen life of the first Adam, so we must be born into the Second Adam's race before we can begin to live His risen life.[13]

Once we have been "born again," we are prepared to participate in a supernatural process that requires us to do three things: first, receive the Living Word, which is God's gracious provision for empowering us to become like Him; second, become aware of the spiritual nature of our mental processes; and third, apply the Written Word, which is God's gracious provision for maintaining this transforming process.

1. Receive the Living Word. Just as none of us were able to will our own conception, gestation, and birth, so none of us have the power to will our spiritual birth.[14] Our will is involved in our conversion, but only as a confirmation of His will. Long before we chose Christ, He chose us.[15] Our new birth is a supernatural expression of His.

Having supernaturally brought us into His family He gives us the supernatural power necessary to become like Him. [16] This does not mean that we *will* become like Him. It only means that we *can*. The supernatural power this transformation requires is God's gift to us, but we must be willing to bring it into our decision-making problem-solving process.

However, if people believe that being lost primarily refers to going to hell when one dies, then once they are saved from that danger, they often show little motivation to make further changes in their lives. While they gladly embrace the eternal safety provided by their new birth, they continue to govern their own lives with little attention given to making Christ Lord of their mental activity.

Such faulty thinking is responsible for many Christians being content to live a carnal life. They trust the second Adam to take them to heaven when they die but they are content to live much like the first Adam while they are on earth. Observing this, a Christian cynic was heard to say, "Then I guess it's not Jesus' fault so many people call themselves Christians."

This is tragic! These believers are missing out on the exciting discovery that their presence can become His presence. Even more tragic, the contradictions between their beliefs and their behavior become a stumbling block that discourages their family and friends from ever discovering Christ as their Savior.

Having blessed us with a supernatural birth into His family, God will not forsake us to our own will and way. He wants us to see the supernatural nature of our mental activity. He wants to give us the supernatural power necessary for applying the discipline of the written Word to our mental activity so we can attain *"the whole measure of the fullness of Christ."*[17]

2. Become spiritually aware of your mental activity

Most people are unaware of the spiritual nature of their mental activity. Over the years this has become obvious to me as I have worked with so many patients who will sit for several seconds staring silently into space fighting a spiritual battle in their mind, screening their thoughts, trying to decide which of them they will share with me. So I will say to them, "What are you thinking about?" And the standard reply is, "Oh, nothing. I'm just thinking."

Then I take the opportunity to explain, "We are never just thinking. Thinking is always an exercise in spiritual warfare." A major part of their treatment consists of helping them learn and apply many of the truths in this book

Become aware of the warfare that is raging for your will in the silent process of your thinking. Urges, fantasies, and ideas stimulated by Satan are clashing with urges, fantasies, and ideas stimulated by Christ. Out of the heat of this battle spiritual impressions will be transformed into physical expressions. The hidden contents of your heart will be revealed in which you choose to do and say.

Our attitudes and behaviors all have their origins in this kind of crucible where divine and demonic urges, fantasies and ideas contend for physical expression through our choices. If we are going to overcome sin we must learn to discern it in our mental activity before we have physically expressed it. After all, a lie doesn't begin when you speak it or adultery doesn't begin when you get in bed with someone other than your spouse. These acts are always preceded by urges, fantasies, and ideas.

The operational definitions for sin and eternal life that were referred to earlier are very helpful in enabling us to discriminate between these two very different sources of our urges, fantasies and ideas. Let's review them. *"Eternal life is an invisible power emanating from Jesus to which the unregenerate are insensitive. It impacts the mind of the regenerate person to stimulate the brain to think in terms of urges, fantasies, and ideas that enhance and develop my divine potential."* On the other hand, *"Sin is an invisible power that emanates from Satan which impacts on my mind to stimulate my brain to think in terms of urges, fantasies and ideas that detract from and destroy my divine potential."*

The fact that this invisible power emanating from Satan stimulates certain urges, fantasies and ideas in my brain, does not mean that I have to physically express them. As long as God helps me to deny them expression they are simply temptations that soon pass from my attention.[18] But if I choose to express one of them it is no longer a part of the invisible spiritual world; I have transformed it into my physical world. It has become a part of my personal history and I must live with the consequences.

A person will always be in prison to sin if he cannot

become aware of it until he has expressed it. For by the time he recognizes he is in a battle, he has already lost the war.

This battle for control of our mental activity occurs at lightning-like speeds. For example, our verbal thoughts flash through our minds at 3,000 to 4,000 words a minute—ten times faster than anyone else can talk to you. This is why trying to change someone by talking with them can be so frustrating. By the time you have spoken 100 words to help them see the benefits of changing they have mounted a silent 1000 word argument for staying the same. And, *until the pain of remaining the same hurts more than the pain of changing they are going to remain the same.* So you may as well save your breath to cool your soup.

We need to be aware that our mental activity is spiritual warfare and no one can win the battle for us from the outside. This is why change has to happen from the inside out. It will never happen from the outside in. God provides us with spiritual weapons that help us win this war. These weapons enable us to discern the spiritual origin of our thoughts, capture those that are not of divine origin and make them obedient to Christ.[19]

3. Apply the written Word. Remember, our presence flows out of those parts of our history we have chosen to store up in our heart over the years.[20] We carry a residue of our yesterdays into our tomorrows. This is why Solomon cautions us to be diligent about what we keep there[21]. The Hebrew word for "keep" in this Proverb conveys the idea of guarding or protecting from an enemy. Satan has a vested interest in contaminating our hearts with poison from our past that paralyzes our present and pollutes our future.

How can we know if there are still infections in our hearts that need to be cleansed by His grace? After all, the human heart is more deceitful than any other thing we have to deal with in life. It is so desperately wicked that only the Lord can know it.[22]

However, if we will expose our hearts to the written Word

God will reveal to us anything there that needs to be surrendered to Him. The importance of Scripture in this sanctifying process cannot be overemphasized.

Being transformed into the presence of Christ involves emptying our hearts of everything we know is not of Him. This is a daily process. Committing David's prayer to memory and repeating it often helps us to be honest about what may be hidden there.. "Search me, O God, and know my heart; test me and know my anxious thoughts. See if there is any offensive way in me, and lead me in the way everlasting."[23]

Scriptures Nourish Our Spirit

In defeating Satan's first temptation, Jesus reminds us that God's word is more essential nourishment for us than bread. [24] If the image of Christ is to thrive in us we must hunger for the Scriptures—just as a newborn baby hungers for milk.[25] Peter reminds us that the promises of Scripture have not been given to help us get things from God. They have been given specifically to enable us to participate in His divine nature.[26]

How do the Scriptures do this? As we familiarize ourselves with them and commit them to memory the Holy Spirit uses them to help us discern more and more accurately the spiritual origins of our urges, fantasies, and ideas. Unfortunately, even though some people have been Christians for years they have not seen the need nor taken the time to become familiar enough with the Bible to be very advanced in this discipline. Although they have been Christians long enough to be able to teach others these skills they are still at the beginner level and not very capable of discerning good and evil in their own mental activity.[27]

The Scriptures are the only reliable tool for identifying the spiritual origins of your urges, fantasies and ideas.[28] If you want to grow more and more into the likeness of Christ, commit the written Word of God to memory. The instruction of the Written Word and the power of the Living Word enable us to develop spiritual control over our urges, fantasies, and ideas so we can subject them to a Biblical test before choosing which to put into action.

Developing Discipline Requires Time and Patience

Two steps are involved in acquiring this kind of spiritual discipline, but they can proceed simultaneously: familiarizing ourselves with the Scriptures and internalizing them; and applying the Scriptures in discerning and disciplining our mental activity. Developing and maintaining this kind of discipline over our mental activity requires diligent practice over time.

I have found three ways of internalizing the Word of God that have been helpful to me: 1. Reading; 2. Hearing; and 3. Memorizing.

1. Reading. As a young man, I realized the importance of reading Scripture. Over the years I have enjoyed a number of approaches to Bible reading. New believers may find it helpful to read through the teachings of Jesus several times. These are found in the Gospels (Matthew, Mark, Luke, and John), the first chapter of Acts and the first four chapters of Revelation. Once you are very familiar with Jesus' teaching you can use them as a commentary for understanding other books of the New Testament. The Book of Acts will provide you with the history of the first century Church. The epistles will expose you to the doctrines and practices of early Christians.

By reading three chapters a day you can read the Bible through in a year. Reading about great characters in the Bible can also be fun. You will be surprised at how familiar you will become with the Scriptures in this process.

2. Hearing. My wife enjoys listening to the Bible on tapes. She bought a player that accommodates two sets of earphones so we can listen together. There are several sound recordings of the Bible on tapes and discs that we have found pleasant to hear.

3. Memorizing. Bible verse memory cards are very helpful for some people. These can be found at any Christian bookstore. Keep several with you at all times. They will provide you with constructive ways to use the time you spend in the waiting rooms of professional people or waiting for family members at shopping malls.

As your knowledge and understanding of Scripture grows, practice screening your mental activity through the Word of God. When the written Word reveals an urge, fantasy, or idea to be coming from Satan you can silently call on the power of the Living Word to strengthen your will so that you can deny it expression.[29] Practice praying to yourself, "Lord, help me not to say this or do this because I want my presence to become Your presence, not the presence of our enemy."

Before long, you will discover that having an urge to do or say something doesn't mean you must do or say it. Ask the Holy Spirit to strengthen your will. Ask Him to increase your tolerance for inner tension so that you don't feel like you are going to burst if you don't say something or do something to relieve the tension. Discover that you can be still and know God is giving you control over your mental processes.

Unfortunately, many Christians never discover the supernatural nature of this process. They try to accomplish this transformation with will power alone. I call them "Boy Scout Christians." Like Boy Scouts, they take an oath, "On my honor I will do my duty and try my best to be like Jesus."

Gerald was like that. He was a well-respected professional man in his community. He taught a large Bible class in his church and served on the board of deacons. But Gerald had a secret. For over twenty years he had been addicted to pornography.

Finally, his wife could not take it any longer. She had struggled with this contradiction in his life all through their marriage. Their sons were growing into their teens and she was fearful that Gerald's problem would become their problem.

It was when she threatened to leave him that Gerald finally got enough courage to be honest with his pastor about what was going on in his life. Gerald felt he was too prominent in his community to be seen locally; so, he commuted several hundred miles by plane to see me.

My heart went out to him as he recalled his twenty year history of spiritual defeat. Tears streamed down his face as he told me how many times and how many different ways he had tried to break free from this bondage. His longest period of abstinence was three months.

He had gone through the, "If you forgive me, Lord I'll never do it again" pledge so many times he couldn't possibly remember them all. His wife loved him, but she didn't respect him.

I explained to him the supernatural approach we take to treating addictions and other emotional problems. I gave him the operational definitions of sin and eternal life. I explained to him that his will was a necessary, but not sufficient component of the treatment process. That is, his will had to be involved in the process, but it was not strong enough to provide the relief he needed. His success would depend on his ability to become aware of the spiritual origin of his lusts and even more aware that the power of "eternal life" in him was greater than the power of "sin."

Gerald had to sort out the difference between his will and the power of "eternal life," but he soon discovered that one was limited and the other was limitless. "I can't believe that I have been in the church all these years and never knew that eternal life was an extension of Christ's life into my life—a real power that can impact my decision-making and my problem-solving. This is the first time I have had any hope that I could finally get this monkey off my back."

Gerald and I worked together almost nine months. When

he had six months of abstinence we celebrated. When he left treatment we both felt he understood his utter dependence on "eternal life" to give him the power to resist temptation that his will alone could not provide.

An opportunity opened up for him in another community which allowed him and his wife to have a new start. I got a warm letter of celebration when he had been free from pornography for a year.

His devotional life has been transformed. He is now aware that thinking is more than neurotransmitters and neuro-hormones doing their "thing." He knows it is spiritual warfare. He is still aware of the enemy's presence, but he knows who the victor is.

Gerald is still teaching a Bible class, but now his most admiring student is his wife. She sees Jesus in Gerald...and so does Gerald.

As your passion for His presence to be expressed in your body grows you will find yourself automatically screening your urges, fantasies and ideas through the filter of God's written Word. You will be aware of One who is greater than you, not only helping you discern the enemy's presence in your mental activity, but also giving you the power to deny him expression. Finally, the Scriptures will become like a mirror reflecting His image to you. They will show you ways He wants you to change so that you can reflect Him more clearly before a world that desperately needs Him. But best of all, you will discover that you don't have to be a "Boy Scout Christian." Your will is involved, but He is the One enabling the process.

When we are willing to be willing He steps into the process and provides the necessary power to make us more like Him. Paul defines this process as "putting off the old self" and putting on the new self."[30] This is how he describes the results, "And we who...reflect the Lord's glory are being transformed into

His likeness with ever increasing glory!"[31]

      This is the coveted imprint we all want to leave on those whose paths cross ours.

FOOTNOTES

[1] John 10:10
[2] Matthew 6:10
[3] Revelation 5:11
[4] Genesis 1:26
[5] Colossians 2:9-10; John 1:16
[6] Mark 8:36-37
[7] I Corinthians 6:13
[8] I Corinthians 6:19
[9] I Corinthians 6:20
[10] Romans 12:1-2
[11] II Corinthians 5:17; I Peter 2:9
[12] John 3:1-8
[13] I Corinthians 15:45-49
[14] John 1:13
[15] John 15:16; Ephesians 1:4
[16] John 1:12
[17] Ephesians 4:13
[18] I Corinthians 10:13
[19] II Corinthians 10:4
[20] Matthew 12:35
[21] Proverbs 4:23
[22] Jeremiah 17:1
[23] Psalms 139:23-24
[24] Matthew 4:4
[25] I Peter 2:2
[26] II Peter 1:4
[27] Hebrews 5:12-14
[28] Hebrews 4:12
[29] Ephesians 3:16-17
[30] Ephesians 4:22-32
[31] II Corinthians 3:18

CHAPTER EIGHT

LASTING
IMPRINTS

When our telephone rang early in January 1992 our family was not prepared to hear what the doctor had to say. Dolores, my first wife, had been fighting non-Hodgkins lymphoma for three years. Early in December she had received the first in her third round of chemotherapy treatments. We had hoped that this would at least buy her more time if not prove to be a step toward remission. The telephone call was from her oncologist.

I could tell from the tone of his voice the news he was about to give me was not good. The treatment not only failed to help Dolores it had actually worsened her condition. She knew this was a possibility when she consented to the treatment. However, there was a twenty percent chance it would help her. For both of us, it was better than no chance, which would have been the result of doing nothing.

The doctor had been thoughtful enough to deliberately withhold this information from us during the holidays so that our family's Christmas memories would not be clouded with such dismally disappointing information. Now we knew that short of a miracle, we would not have another Christmas together.

Dolores asked the doctor how much time she had. He told us that he was not very good at such predictions, but said she probably had less than three months. There is no way to understand how such news affects a family unless you have been there. And, if you have been there you don't need a description.

Actually Dolores lived six months longer. These were not easy months for her, but we all were amazed at how she managed them. Even though she was a woman of great faith, she had battled anxiety and depression much of her life. However, her faith gave her the courage and strength to face the challenge of death in a way that was an inspiration to us all. It was as though she was comforted by the gradual dawning of an eternal reality she had believed in all her life.

During her last two weeks she had hospice care twenty-four hours a day. Two of the three ladies who tended her were Christians. The one who was not was surprised by the way our family dealt with death. She said she had never seen a family face death with such composure and hope.

Dolores loved to listen to Scripture tapes. Her favorite passage was the fourth and fifth chapters of second Corinthians and we played them for her several times a day.

She lost consciousness three days before she went to be with the Lord. However, when the children were there we would still play those passages, join hands, and sing songs about heaven: *When The Roll Is Called Up Yonder*, *I'll Fly Away*, *Won't It Be Wonderful There*; and, *When We All Get To Heaven.*

These times were filled with mixed emotions. There was the sadness and agonizing grief of anticipating our severe personal loss. I was losing my wife. The children were losing their mother. Home would never be the same. But there was also an intense awareness of the Lord's presence. This left no doubt in any of our minds that death is a spiritual experience. And, as paradoxical as it seems, there was something undeniably precious about those times.[1]

About seven o'clock on Friday morning after we had finished singing and praying the family went downstairs for a quick breakfast. We just had just poured the coffee when the tiny Puerto Rican nurse who was with Dolores at the time came downstairs to inform us in her unforgettable Spanish accent, "Dolores has just slipped into the presence of the Lord."

We rushed back upstairs hoping to have one last moment with her, but she was gone. Her body was still there, lying motionless on the bed, but the person whose presence was expressed through that body was gone. In moments like this the difference between the person's visible body and the invisible presence produced by their spirit and soul is profoundly real.

The family never talked about Dolores being alone when she died because we all knew she wasn't. The same Great Shepherd who was with David was with her.[2] No one who knows Him will die alone.[3]

We Leave Our Imprint On Others

In the days following the funeral I began to go through the sacks of mail Dolores had received during her illness. There must have been two hundred or more cards and letters from men and women of all ages. She had taught them in Sunday school, taken food to their families during long labor strikes or periods of unemployment, cleaned their homes when they were too sick to do it for themselves, brought them to church if they couldn't find a way...in one way or another Dolores had left her imprint on them...and they had never forgotten it.

I remember one letter in particular. It read,

"You probably won't remember me, but when I was a ten year old girl you were my Sunday school teacher. There were three sets of children in our home because my Mom had been married four times, but you treated me as other children whose parents were still married to each other.

"I just want to let you know what an impact you had on my life. I looked forward to your class every week. You made all of us kids feel loved. I always said when I grew up I wanted to be like you. Well, I have my own grandchildren now and I just hope I can have the same kind of influence on them and their friends that you had on me. I'm praying for you. God bless you!"

Others Imprint Our Lives

If you were going to write letters to just two people who left the most lasting imprint on you during the formative years of your life who would they be? A family member, a neighbor, a school teacher, a friend, someone you worked with, your pastor... who would they be?

I would find this to be a difficult assignment because so many people left lasting imprints on my life. I can still hear my maternal grandmother crying and praying for me. She was a great intercessor. Many times as I passed the room where she was praying I would stop and listen until I heard my name. Only God knows where I would be or what I would be doing if it weren't for her prayers. I was all that was left of my mother, her baby daughter, so she poured herself into her prayers for me.

I also have wonderful memories of spending the night with my maternal grandparents and sleeping with my granddad. Before we drifted off to sleep I would ask him to tell me a story. He would recall stories from his hunting days when he lived in a lumber camp in western Pennsylvania where he worked as a woodsman. How factual those stories were is not important. They helped me overcome my fear of the dark and put me to sleep.

Then there was my university academic counselor who gave me the confidence I needed to tackle college when I was twenty-nine years old. As a late bloomer, I wasn't sure how I would do in graduate school, but with his encouragement I went on to earn an M.A. and a Ph.D. in four years.

However, if I were only going to write two letters, one would go to my aunt who raised me. I would not address her as my aunt because that is not the way I felt about her. She was the only Mother I ever knew, so that's what I would call her in my letter. Whether she was chasing me with a switch yelling, "Are you going to do that again?" or, tucking me in bed at night with a kiss, I knew she loved me. She was one of the godliest persons I have ever known. I am serving the Lord today because of my grandmother's prayers and my Mom's life. I still wonder what would have happened to me if she had not married my dad and raised me for her sister. She is with the Lord now, but I'm glad I took the time to let her know how much I loved her while she was still with us.

The other person who would get a letter from me is the pastor who mentored me during my early years in the ministry. He came to pastor my home church at a critical time in my life. He and his wife had lost their only child in infancy. Had the boy lived, he would have been exactly my age. I'm sure our relationship met needs that both of us had at the time.

The practical lessons he taught me about the ministry are still helpful to me. He would say, "Don't waste your money on sermon books. Read the books the men read who wrote the sermon books." This germinal statement alone has been responsible for driving me to original sources when delving into any subject in depth.

He taught me how to make a hospital visit, pray for the sick, conduct a funeral, make a home visit, lead a communion service, and make water baptism meaningful for people. I learned the importance of parliamentary procedure from him and how to use it in business sessions. He also stressed the importance of studying theology and giving it a prominent place in my preaching.

Much of this was learned on the golf course or in the course of making hospital visits together. I have had several opportunities to express my appreciation to him, but one more letter wouldn't hurt.

Of course, I have not mentioned everyone who left a positive imprint on my life. And I have deliberately chosen not to include any whose scars I still bear. They were forgiven long ago and I wouldn't want what I write here to bring any pain to them.

For better or for worse, we all leave our imprints on each

other. As you look back over your life, who are the people who bear your imprint? Has your imprint helped them? In the course of life we all hurt others. The purpose of this reflection is not to paralyze us with guilt, but to make us aware that we have the power to help others (or hurt them) with our presence.

Paul was aware of the pain he had brought into the lives of hundreds of Christians. He had imprisoned and executed many Christian men, making widows of their wives and orphans of their children.[4] No doubt this helped him absorb the pain that he later suffered at the hands of others for the sake of the Gospel.[5] However, he did not allow guilt from the past to cripple his present pursuit of God's highest and best for his life.[6]

It is impossible to live without hurting others or being hurt by others. However, the more aware we become of what other people feel when they are around us the less likely we are to inflict pain on them and the more understanding we will be when they inflict pain on us.

Your Presence Is Not Spiritually Neutral

When someone is in the same room with you, you are not only physically sharing the same room, but you are also spiritually sharing the same space. Each of you is spiritually impacting the other...leaving your imprint on the other...for better or for worse.

When one of you leaves the room, that person takes his or her presence with them. If the presence of the person who has left has been offensive, relief will come to the person who remains, but if the presence of the person who left is pleasant they will be missed. Thus, an invisible imprint is made. Making these kinds of observations about the presence of another person can teach you a great deal about your own presence and how it is affecting other people.

The body was created to house God's presence. The first Adam refused to allow God to live in his body. So God sent Jesus, His only begotten Son, as the Second Adam to begin a new race.

Jesus lived the perfect human life and surrendered it to God as a sacrifice for our sins. When we accept Christ's death as the sacrifice God requires for our sins, God forgives us, the miracle of the new birth takes place and the life of Christ begins to be expressed through us.

The miracle of grace that brings Christ's presence into my body gives me the power to become a physical expression of Jesus to those with whom I live. Jesus wants me to leave His imprint on the lives of others. I do this through my attitudes, words, and deeds. This is what being a Christian is about. Christ's life is an attractive life. As we express that life others will be attracted to Him through us. In heaven we will rejoice with all who are there because they saw the invisible imprint of Christ's life in us.

FOOTNOTES

[1] Psalms 116:15
[2] Psalms 23:4
[3] Matthew 28:20
[4] I Timothy 1:13-16
[5] II Timothy 3:10-14
[6] Philippians 3:12-14
[7] Matthew 5:16